Endorsements

"There has been a terrible misreading of modern missions, and it's this: our heroes on the mission field were lone rangers who pulled themselves up by their spiritual bootstraps to take the gospel to the lost. Finally, that caricature has exploded thanks to Michael A.G. Haykin, who demonstrates that the founder of modern missions himself, William Carey, depended not only on God but on close friendships to bring the good news to unreached peoples. Through the art of biography, Haykin reminds Christians today that fellowship is not only key to the Christian life but is essential to the Christian mission. The devil can take down a solo Christian, but he cannot penetrate a band of Christian brothers who link arms to advance the gospel."

—Dr. Matthew Barrett
Associate professor of Christian theology
Midwestern Baptist Theological Seminary, Kansas City, Mo.

"Michael Haykin's *The Missionary Fellowship of William Carey* is among the best I have read on William Carey. Haykin calls our attention to a dimension that ought to be seriously considered, remembered, and fostered in the context of any Christian ministry. And William Carey's successful but stressful life is an outstanding illustration of it. What would have happened to Carey, the work in India, and his influence worldwide without his friends? This book ought to be read and discussed not only among missionaries, mission agencies, and mission organizations worldwide; it should be studied in any ecclesiastical and ministerial context."

—Dr. Elias Dos Santos Medeiros
Harriet Barbour Professor of Missions
Reformed Theological Seminary, Jackson, Miss.

"Pioneers such as William Carey gave birth to the modern missionary movement. It was Carey's sense of evangelistic passion, set upon a clear foundation of biblical truth and confidence in the gospel, that compelled him to leave the safe confines of England and go to India. The full harvest of William Carey's ministry will be known only in eternity. This new biography of Carey is a compelling presentation of the man, his theology, and his deep love for the nations. Haykin's treatment is compelling, is warm-hearted, and will point beyond Carey to the Savior he loved so deeply."

—Dr. R. Albert Mohler Jr.
President and Joseph Emerson Brown
Professor of Christian Theology
The Southern Baptist Theological Seminary, Louisville, Ky.

"Christian fellowship, friendship, and mission are inexorably linked. One cannot claim to be on God's mission and live in isolation; in fact, any missional effort devoid of a community of friends and coworkers is vanity. I am thankful for Michael Haykin's work reminding us—as Westerners—of the beauty of friendship with like-minded people and how this principle was visible in the life of William Carey, the father of modern mission. This book will be a blessing to those who are students of history, and there are many lessons to be learned in its pages that will help Christians be multipliers of God's mission and ministry."

—Dr. Ed Stetzer
Billy Graham Distinguished Chair of Church,
Mission, and Evangelism
Wheaton College, Wheaton, Ill.

The Missionary Fellowship *of*

William Carey

The Long Line of Godly Men Profiles

Series editor, Steven J. Lawson

The Expository Genius of John Calvin
by Steven J. Lawson

The Unwavering Resolve of Jonathan Edwards
by Steven J. Lawson

The Mighty Weakness of John Knox
by Douglas Bond

The Gospel Focus of Charles Spurgeon
by Steven J. Lawson

The Heroic Boldness of Martin Luther
by Steven J. Lawson

The Poetic Wonder of Isaac Watts
by Douglas Bond

The Evangelistic Zeal of George Whitefield
by Steven J. Lawson

The Trinitarian Devotion of John Owen
by Sinclair B. Ferguson

The Daring Mission of William Tyndale
by Steven J. Lawson

The Passionate Preaching of Martyn Lloyd-Jones
by Steven J. Lawson

The Missionary Fellowship of William Carey
by Michael A.G. Haykin

The Affectionate Theology of Richard Sibbes
by Mark Dever

A Long Line of Godly Men Profile

The Missionary Fellowship *of*

William Carey

MICHAEL A.G. HAYKIN

The Missionary Fellowship of William Carey
© 2018 by Michael A.G. Haykin

Published by Ligonier Ministries
421 Ligonier Court, Sanford, FL 32771
Ligonier.org

Printed in Harrisonburg, Virginia
Lakeside Book Company
0000922
First edition, second printing

ISBN 978-1-64289-008-2 (Hardcover)
ISBN 978-1-64289-009-9 (ePub)
ISBN 978-1-64289-010-5 (Kindle)

Cover design: Steven Noble
Interior design and typeset: Katherine Lloyd, The DESK

Scripture quotations are taken from the Holy Bible, King James Version.
Public domain.

Some material in this book is adapted from Michael A.G. Haykin, "'A Wretched,
Poor, and Helpless Worm': The Life and Legacy of William Carey (1761–1834),"
Fontes: The Writings of Michael A.G. Haykin (blog), accessed February 27, 2005,
http://haykin.luxpub.com:80/bb-careybiography.html (site discontinued).

The Library of Congress has cataloged the Reformation Trust edition as follows:

Names: Haykin, Michael A. G., author.
Title: The missionary fellowship of William Carey / Michael A.G. Haykin.
Description: Orlando, FL : Reformation Trust Publishing, a division of
    Ligonier Ministries, [2018] | Includes bibliographical references and index.
Identifiers: LCCN 2018019028 (print) | LCCN 2018041499 (ebook) | ISBN
    9781642890099 (E-book) | ISBN 9781642890105 (E-book mobi) | ISBN
    9781642890082
Subjects: LCSH: Carey, William, 1761-1834. | Carey, William,
    1761-1834--Friends and associates. | Missionaries--England--Biography. |
    Baptists--England--Biography. | Missionaries--India--Biography. |
    Baptists--India--Biography.
Classification: LCC BV3269.C3 (ebook) | LCC BV3269.C3 H39 2018 (print) | DDC
    266/.61092 [B] --dc23
LC record available at https://lccn.loc.gov/2018019028

To three dear friends:

Peter and Anna Pikkert—
"plodders" by grace like Carey—
and Haitham John Issak,
a lover of Christ like Carey

TABLE OF CONTENTS

Followers Worthy to Be Followed

Down through the centuries, God has raised up a long line of godly men whom He has mightily used at strategic moments in church history. These valiant individuals have come from all walks of life, from the ivy-covered halls of elite schools to the dusty back rooms of tradesmen's shops. They have arisen from all points of this world, from highly visible venues in densely populated cities to obscure hamlets in remote locations. Yet despite these diverse differences, these pivotal figures have held in common those virtues that remain nonnegotiable.

Each man possessed an unwavering faith in the Lord Jesus Christ. But more than that, each of these stalwarts of the faith held deep convictions in the God-exalting truths known as the doctrines of grace. Though they differed in secondary matters of theology, they stood shoulder to shoulder in embracing these biblical teachings that magnify the sovereign grace of God in salvation. These spiritual leaders stood upon and upheld the foundational truth that "salvation is of the Lord" (Ps. 3:8; Jonah 2:9).

Any survey of church history reveals that those who have embraced these biblical Reformed truths have been granted extraordinary confidence in their God. Far from paralyzing these spiritual giants, the doctrines of grace kindled within their hearts a reverential awe for God that humbled their souls before His throne. The truths of divine sovereignty emboldened these men to rise up and advance the cause of Christ on the earth. With an enlarged vision for the expansion of His kingdom upon the earth, they stepped forward boldly to accomplish the work of ten, even twenty men. They arose with wings like eagles and soared over their times. The doctrines of grace ignited them to serve God in their divinely appointed hour of history, leaving a godly inheritance for future generations.

This Long Line of Godly Men Profiles series highlights key figures in the agelong procession of these sovereign-grace men. The purpose of this series is to introduce you to these significant figures and explore how they used their God-given gifts and abilities to impact their times for the work of Christ. Because they were courageous followers of the Lord, their examples are worthy of our emulation today.

This volume focuses on the pioneering missionary William Carey. Celebrated during his own lifetime for his evangelistic efforts on the Indian subcontinent, Carey risked everything to take the gospel to people who lived in darkness. He also put the lie to the notion that Calvinism and missions don't mix. Far from holding to a view of God's sovereignty that sees no place for missions and evangelism, Carey was consumed with passion for God's power to convert sinners as revealed in the gospel. In his efforts, he was joined by a stalwart group of similarly committed friends, whose cooperation in the mission of God should inspire us all to join hands with our Christian brothers and sisters as we pass through this earthly life.

I want to thank the publishing team at Reformation Trust for their commitment to this Long Line of Godly Men Profiles series. I remain thankful for the ongoing influence of my former professor and revered friend, Dr. R.C. Sproul. I must also express my gratitude to Chris Larson, who is so instrumental in overseeing this series. Finally, I am grateful to Dr. Michael Haykin for authoring this volume and helping to introduce William Carey to a new generation.

May the Lord use this book to energize and embolden a new generation of believers to bring its witness for Jesus Christ upon this world for God. Through this profile of William Carey, may you be strengthened to walk in a manner worthy of your calling. May you be zealous in your study of the written Word of God for the exaltation of Christ and the advance of His kingdom.

Soli Deo gloria!
—Steven J. Lawson
Series editor

Understanding William Carey

For English-speaking people, the eighteenth century was an era of highly significant achievements. Through conquest and exploration, they established themselves as the masters of a far-flung empire that encircled the globe. It was in the middle of this century that British troops under the command of Robert Clive (1725–74) defeated a French army in India at the Battle of Plassey, which paved the way for the British conquest of Bengal and later all of India. Two years later, on September 13, 1759, General James Wolfe (1727–59) defeated the French general Louis Joseph Montcalm (1712–59) at the Battle of the Plains of Abraham, then outside the walls of the city of Quebec. Though Wolfe was killed in this engagement, the British victory meant the end of French rule in Canada. Within another decade, the British naval officer Captain James Cook (1728–79) entered upon his world-changing discoveries in the South Pacific, mapping the coastlines of New Zealand and Australia.[1]

Running parallel to this empire building by the British, though distinct from it, came the kingdom building by English-speaking missionaries. Up until the latter part of the eighteenth century, evangelical Christianity was primarily confined to Northern Europe and the Atlantic seaboard of North America. But suddenly, in the last decade of the century, these evangelicals launched out from these two regions and began to establish churches throughout Asia, Africa, and Australasia. At the heart of this missionary movement was William Carey (1761–1834), who has come to be known as "the founder of modern missions," a description that was especially dear to the Victorians.[2] To them, he was an iconic missionary pioneer.

"I Am a Plodder"

This celebrity status accorded to Carey actually began in his lifetime. "Such a man as Carey is more to me than bishop or archbishop: he is an apostle," the evangelical Anglican John

---

1 For an excellent overall account of this empire-building by the British, see Kirsten McKenzie, "Britain: Ruling the Waves" in Robert Aldrich, *The Age of Empires* (London: Thames & Hudson, 2007), 128–51.

2 See, for example, John Taylor, ed., *Biographical and Literary Notices of William Carey, D.D.* (Northampton, England: Dryden, Taylor & Son/London: Alexander & Shepheard, 1886), 86; William Edward Winks, *Lives of Illustrious Shoemakers* (London: Sampson Low, Marston and Co., 1882), 147; George Smith, *The Life of William Carey: Shoemaker & Missionary* (London: J.M. Dent & Sons/New York: E.P. Dutton & Co., 1909), 315.

Newton (1725–1807) once expressed. On another occasion, Newton wrote that he did not look for miracles in his own day on the order of those done in the Apostolic era. Yet, he went on, "if God were to work one in our day, I should not wonder if it were in favor of Dr. Carey."[3] Similarly, in 1826, when two missionaries by the names of George Bennet and Daniel Tyerman happened to visit Carey in India (by that time, he had been laboring there for more than thirty years), they were struck by what they later called his "apostolic appearance."[4]

But Carey's opinion of himself was quite different. He once told his nephew Eustace Carey (1791–1855): "I am a plodder, it is true. I have no genius, but I can plod."[5] In other words, Carey saw his achievements not as the work of an inspired Apostle but as the product of grit, gumption, and, he would have wanted to add, God's grace. Carey was quite conscious that he did not merit being decked out with a halo like some medieval saint, something that later evangelical tradition—following Newton's lead?—has in essence done. Carey was convinced that he had simply done his duty as a servant of Christ.[6]

---

3   *The Autobiography of William Jay*, eds. George Redford and John Angell James (1854; repr., Edinburgh, Scotland: Banner of Truth, 1974), 275; S. Pearce Carey, *William Carey* (London: Hodder and Stoughton, [1923]), 134.

4   Tom Hiney, *On the Missionary Trail* (London: Chatto & Windus, 2000), 222.

5   Cited in Francis Wayland, "Introductory Essay" to Eustace Carey, *Memoir of William Carey, D.D.* (Boston: Gould, Kendall, and Lincoln, 1836), xiv–xv.

6   A. Christopher Smith, "The Legacy of William Carey," *International Bulletin of Missionary Research* 16, no. 1 (January 1992): 2.

A Solitary Pioneer?

The lionization of Carey has depicted him as something of a solitary pioneer, someone whose remarkable character triumphed over both lackadaisical Christianity in England and various tremendous obstacles on the field in India. Consider for a moment a text written on Carey by Francis Wayland (1796–1865), probably the leading Baptist theologian in the Northern United States during Carey's lifetime. As president of the Baptist school Brown University in Providence, R.I., from 1827 to 1855, Wayland provided hearty support of the modern missionary movement that was an important factor in stimulating a missions-mindedness among Baptist churches in America. As a result of his missionary passion, he was eventually asked to write the authorized biography of the American Baptist missionary Adoniram Judson (1788–1850), who was baptized as a believer by Carey's coworker William Ward (1769–1823). This two-volume work sold an amazing twenty-six thousand copies in 1853, its first year of publication, a total that would make it a best seller even in today's Christian book market.

An earlier missionary tract by Wayland was his "Introductory Essay" to the first American edition of Eustace Carey's *Memoir of William Carey*, the earliest major biography of William Carey, which appeared in 1836.[7] Wayland's

---

7   Wayland, "Introductory Essay," ix–xxii. A second American edition appeared in 1837, published in Hartford, Conn., with an introductory essay by Jeremiah Chaplin.

essay occupies fourteen pages in the book. Wayland lists the numerous hurdles that Carey had to overcome to become an ideal missionary, among them the lack of support by fellow Christians in England and the overt opposition of the East India Company, which essentially ruled as a governing body in India. And Carey looked in vain for support from his first wife, Dorothy (1756–1807), for, Wayland says, she was "querulous and unreasonable, capricious and obstinate," and eventually became insane.[8] For Wayland, it was the calling of William Carey "to be a pioneer, and to act alone" that dominated his view of the Baptist missionary.[9] However, Carey was, above all things, a team player, but one never gets this impression from reading Wayland's essay.

"A Little Band of Brothers"

Devoted friends in England—Andrew Fuller (1754–1815), John Ryland Jr. (1753–1825), John Sutcliff (1752–1814), and Samuel Pearce (1766–99)—and in India—William Ward and Joshua Marshman (1768–1837)—none of whom are mentioned by Wayland in his essay, were utterly essential to Carey's achievements as a missionary on the Indian subcontinent. In fact, collegiality is ever central to times of spiritual blessing in the history of the Christian faith. As James Davison Hunter argues in his book *To Change the World: The Irony, Tragedy,*

---

8   Wayland, "Introductory Essay," xx.

9   Wayland, "Introductory Essay," xxii.

and Possibility of Christianity in the Late Modern World, the "great man of history" view, namely, that "the history of the world is but the biography of great men," is wrong.[10] Rather, "the key actor in history is not individual genius but rather the network [of individuals and friends] and the new institutions that are created out of those networks." Hunter thus maintains that "charisma and genius and their cultural consequences do not exist outside of networks of similarly oriented people and similarly aligned institutions."[11]

In the history of the church, there are numerous illustrations of the truth of Hunter's thesis. For instance, there is the Pauline circle, the group of men, including Timothy and Titus, who gave up whatever ambitions they had for their own lives to join the Apostle Paul in the glorious work of planting churches throughout the ancient Mediterranean world. There are the Cappadocian Fathers—Basil of Caesarea (c. 329–79), his brother Gregory of Nyssa (c. 335–c. 395), and Gregory of Nazianzus (c. 329–89)—who employed their gifts and calling to bring a close to the Arian controversy and give the church a universal grammar for speaking about the triune God. In the mid-sixteenth century, John Calvin and his circle of friends, including such men as William Farel (1489–1565) and Pierre Viret (1511–71), were on the cutting edge in pushing forward the Reformation. And a superb example of Hunter's

---

10 James Davison Hunter, *To Change the World: The Irony, Tragedy, and Possibility of Christianity in the Late Modern World* (Oxford, England: Oxford University Press, 2010), 38.

11 Hunter, *To Change the World*, 38.

thesis is Carey's network of friends, who played a key role in the renewal of the English Baptist community in the late eighteenth century as well as in the launching of the modern missionary movement. Christopher Anderson (1782–1852), a Scottish Baptist leader who became a close friend of a number of those who were centrally involved in these momentous events, reckoned

> that in order to much good being done, co-operation, the result of undissembled love, is absolutely necessary; and I think that if God in his tender mercy would take me as one of but a very few whose hearts he will unite as the heart of one man—since all the watchmen cannot see eye to eye—might I be but one of a little band of brothers who should do so, and who should leave behind them a proof of how much may be accomplished in consequence of the union of only a few upon earth in spreading Christianity, oh how should I rejoice and be glad! In order to such a union, however, I am satisfied that the cardinal virtues, and a share of what may be considered as substantial excellence of character, are absolutely necessary, and hence the importance of the religion which we possess being of that stamp which will promote these. Such a union in modern times existed in [Andrew] Fuller, [John] Sutcliff, [Samuel] Pearce, [William] Carey, and [John] Ryland. They were men of self-denying habits, dead

to the world, to fame, and to popular applause, of deep and extensive views of divine truth, and they had such an extended idea of what the Kingdom of Christ ought to have been in the nineteenth century, that they, as it were, vowed and prayed, and gave themselves no rest. You . . . know the result.[12]

For much of the eighteenth century, far too many Particular or Calvinistic Baptist churches in England, Wales, and Ireland were moribund and without vision for the future or passion for the salvation of the lost at home or abroad.[13] Definite tendencies toward hyper-Calvinism, an introspective piety that was in part a reaction to the Enlightenment of that era, and an inability to discern God's hand at work in the Calvinistic Methodist revivals of their day, as well as various social and political factors, were central in their decline. By the first decade of the next century, however, the low-burning embers in their churches had been fanned into white-hot flame as this Baptist community became a world leader in the foreign missionary enterprise, an enterprise that became identified with one name in particular, that of William Carey. But Carey did not accomplish this alone.

---

12 Christopher Anderson, letter, September 7, 1822, in Hugh Anderson, *The Life and Letters of Christopher Anderson* (Edinburgh, Scotland: W.P. Kennedy, 1854), 379.

13 They were called "Particular" due to their commitment to particular redemption. The other group of Baptists in England, the General Baptists, were Arminian and so called because of their belief in general redemption. A third, much smaller group of Baptists, the Seventh Day Baptists, were Calvinistic, but worshiped on Saturday, the seventh day.

There is little doubt that Carey's friendship with a number of like-minded Baptist pastors and missionaries was indispensable to the transformative impact of his life. These men took the time to think and reflect together, as well as to encourage one another and pray together. "An aversion to the same errors, a predilection for the same authors, with a concern for the cause of Christ at home and abroad"[14] bound these men together in a friendship that was a significant catalyst for both revival and mission. With no friends in high places and virtually no financial reserves, this small group of men, believing God that their Christian faith was not meant for Westerners alone, committed itself to sending Carey (and later others) to India and Southeast Asia, and then, in the years that followed, yet others to the West Indies and West Africa. And so began in earnest the globalization of the Christian faith.

A FOCUS ON FRIENDSHIP

The chapters that follow examine Carey's network of friends so as to help us better understand some of the roots of Carey's achievements. While this book does follow the course of Carey's life, it is not an exhaustive biography by any means. Certain areas of Carey's life are passed over due to this focus

---

14 John Ryland Jr., *The Indwelling and Righteousness of Christ No Security against Corporal Death, but the Source of Spiritual and Eternal Life* (London: W. Button & Son, 1815), 35–36. These words are actually used by John Ryland Jr. of his friendship with Andrew Fuller, but they can also be applied to the friendship among all of these men.

on friendship. In particular, more space is given to the formation of his circle of friends in England than of that in India. This is not because the former is more important but due to the constraints of space and the desire not to be overly repetitive. The goal of this book, then, is to display the way that friendship was central to Carey's life. It is my hope that Carey will also be a model for us in this regard, for our culture is not one that provides great encouragement for the nurture and development of deep, long-lasting, and satisfying friendships. True friendships take time and sacrifice, and Western culture in the early twenty-first century is a busy world that as a rule is far more interested in receiving and possessing than sacrificing and giving.[15]

Roger Scruton, a conservative public commentator and philosopher who specializes in aesthetics, has rightly noted that Westerners "are living through . . . a decline in real friendship."[16] What is especially disturbing about this fact is that so much of Western Christianity is little different from its culture. C.S. Lewis wrote an ingenious little book titled *The Screwtape Letters*, a remarkable commentary on spiritual warfare from the point of view of our enemy. In it, there is one letter from the senior devil, Screwtape, to his nephew Wormwood in which Screwtape rejoices over the fact that "in modern Christian writings" there is to be found "few of the

---

15 Diogenes Allen, *Love: Christian Romance, Marriage, Friendship* (Cambridge, Mass.: Cowley, 1987), 45–46.

16 Roger Scruton, "Staving Off Despair: On the Use and Abuse of Pessimism for Life," *Standpoint* (September 2010), 36, col. 1.

old warnings about Worldly Vanities, the Choice of Friends, and the Value of Time."[17] Regardless of whether Lewis is right with regard to a scarcity of twentieth-century Christian literature about "Worldly Vanities" and "the Value of Time," he is undoubtedly correct when it comes to the topic of friendship.

But it has not always been so among Christians. This small study seeks to tell a different story, and so illustrate Proverbs 27:17 as it might literally be rendered: "Iron sharpens iron, and a man sharpens his friend's face."

---

17 *The Screwtape Letters*, letter 10, in *The Best of C.S. Lewis* (Washington, D.C.: Canon, 1969), 43.

Chapter One

The Early Years
of William Carey

Carey was born to poor parents, Edmund Carey (d. 1816) and Elizabeth Wells (d. 1787), in 1761 in a tiny village called Paulerspury in the county of Northamptonshire, England. Edmund Carey was a weaver who worked at a handloom in his own cottage to produce a type of woolen cloth known in the district as "tammy." When Carey was six years of age, his father was appointed the parish clerk of Paulerspury as well as the schoolmaster of the village. According to William Cowper (1731–1800), the evangelical hymn writer, the parish clerk had to "pronounce the Amen to prayers and announce the sermon"; lead the chants and responses during the service; keep the church register of baptisms, marriages, and burials; chase "dogs out of church"; and force "unwilling youngsters in."[1] Thus, young William was regularly taken to church. Of this early acquaintance with the Church of England, Carey later wrote:

> Having been accustomed from my infancy to read the Scriptures, I had a considerable acquaintance therewith, especially with the historical parts. I . . . have no doubt but the constant reading of the Psalms, Lessons, etc. in the parish church, which I was obliged to attend regularly, tended to furnish my mind with a general Scripture knowledge. [But] of real experimental religion I scarcely heard anything till I was fourteen years of age.[2]

A Passion for Flowers

Also living in Paulerspury was William's uncle, Peter Carey. Peter had served with General James Wolfe in Canada during the French and Indian War (part of the Seven Years' War) and had seen action at the British capture of the citadel of Quebec in 1759, two years before William was born. Peter subsequently returned to England and worked in Paulerspury as a gardener. His tales of Canada and his experiences there almost

---

1   Mary Drewery, *William Carey: A Biography* (London: Hodder and Stoughton, 1978), 10.

2   Eustace Carey, *Memoir of William Carey, D.D.* (London: Jackson and Walford, 1836), 7.

certainly awakened in young William an unquenchable interest in far-off lands.

Peter also implanted in young William a love of gardens
and flowers that remained with him all of his life. William's
younger sister Mary (1767–1842) later recalled: "He often
took me over the dirtiest roads to get at a plant or an insect.
He never walked out, I think, . . . without observation on the
hedges as he passed; and when he took up a plant of any kind
he always observed it with care."[3] Years later, when Carey was
established in India, he had five acres of garden under cultivation. Cultivating this garden served as a welcome means of
relaxation amid the stresses and strains of ministry in India. It
was of this garden that his son Jonathan later remarked that
"here he [i.e., his father] enjoyed his most pleasant moments
of secret meditation and devotion."[4]

THE WITNESS OF A FRIEND: JOHN WARR

So much did young Carey love gardening that he wanted to
become a gardener like his uncle Peter. At this point in his life,
however, Carey suffered from a skin disease that made it very
painful for him to spend large amounts of time in the full sun. It
is interesting to note that when Carey went to India, he would
spend a considerable amount of time in the sun, but with no
recurrence of this skin disease. And so, in his mid-teens, his

---

3   Carey, *Memoir of William Carey*, 25.

4   Carey, *Memoir of William Carey*, 398.

father apprenticed him to a shoemaker by the name of Clarke Nichols, who lived in Piddington, about seven miles away from his home. In time, Carey became quite good at making shoes, as he himself once noted in a letter to John Ryland.[5]

A number of Carey's biographers have maintained, however, that Carey was not a very good shoemaker. An incident when he was in his forties may have given rise to this perception. He happened to be dining with the British governor-general of India in Calcutta when an officer at the table made an impertinent inquiry of one of the aides-de-camp whether it was true that Carey had once been a shoemaker. Carey happened to overhear the question, and he immediately piped up and said, "No, sir; only a cobbler!"[6] While a shoemaker makes shoes, which obviously requires skilled craftsmanship, a cobbler merely repairs them. Though they are often regarded as synonymous, it is a mistake to confuse the two designations. Of course, a shoemaker can repair shoes when necessity demands it. But Carey's remark reveals the meekness and humility that were dominant aspects of his life as he matured in Christ.

This apprenticeship was to have very significant consequences for William, for one of his fellow apprentices was a Christian. His name was John Warr.[7] He was a Congregationalist and was used of God to bring Carey to Christ. It was

---

5   Carey, *Memoir of William Carey*, 8–9. See also William Edward Winks, *Lives of Illustrious Shoemakers* (London: Sampson Low, Marston and Co., 1882), 147.

6   Winks, *Lives of Illustrious Shoemakers*, 151.

7   On Warr, see S. Pearce Carey, *William Carey*, 8th ed. (London: Carey, 1934), 28–32.

known for a long time that Carey's salvation had come partly as the result of the witness of one of his fellow apprentices. Until the First World War, however, the name of this apprentice had been completely lost. During the war, Warr's name was found in one of Carey's letters that had only then come to light.[8] It is a powerful illustration of how the faithful witness of one believer can have immense consequences.

At first, when Warr spoke with Carey about Christ, Carey resisted the force of his arguments. Carey was the product of a staunch Anglican home and had come to despise anyone who was not a member of this denomination. As Thomas Scott (1747–1821), an evangelical Anglican minister whose preaching was a great help to Carey at one point in his life, commented concerning the Anglican disdain for Dissenters (that is, Baptists and Congregationalists): "We imbibe this prejudice with the first rudiments of instruction, and are taught by our whole education to consider it as meritorious."[9] But as Warr continued to witness to Carey, the latter felt "a growing uneasiness and stings of conscience gradually increasing." Warr lent him books that began to effect a change in his thinking but which also increased his "inward uneasiness." Warr also persuaded him to attend a prayer meeting with him in the nearby village of Hackleton, where a number of Congregationalists gathered midweek for prayer and Bible study. Carey subsequently tried to reform his life—to give up

8   Pearce Carey, *William Carey*, x.
9   Thomas Scott, *The Force of Truth* (Edinburgh, Scotland: Banner of Truth, 1984), 85.

lying and swearing and to take up prayer. But, he later said, he had no idea that "nothing but a complete change of heart" could do him any real and lasting good.[10]

It is interesting that Carey mentioned swearing as one of the major sins that dogged his life before his conversion. Other Europeans in the eighteenth century often noted that the English in general were addicted to swearing. Even cultured, upper-class women habitually swore. When John Newton, for example, was converted in 1748, he observed that he was "freed from the habit of swearing which seems to have been deeply rooted in me as a second nature."[11]

THE IMPACT OF SIN

Coupled with Warr's testimony was an important lesson that young Carey learned from a traumatic incident that took place at Christmas 1777. It was the custom for apprentices at that time of the year to be given small amounts of money from the tradespeople with whom their masters had business. Carey had to go to Northampton to make some purchases for his master as well as for himself. He visited one particular shop, that of a man named Hall, who was an ironmonger—that is, a hardware dealer. Hall jokingly gave young Carey a counterfeit shilling for his personal gift. Hall intended to make it up to

---

10 Pearce Carey, *William Carey*, 30.
11 John Newton, *Out of the Depths: The Autobiography of John Newton* (New Canaan, Conn.: Keats, 1981), 68.

him after Christmas, but this was his idea of Christmas merriment. When Carey discovered the worthless coin, he decided, not without some qualms of conscience, to pass it off to his employer. Appropriating a good shilling from the money that Nichols had given him, he included the counterfeit shilling among the change for his master. On the way back to Piddington, he even prayed that if God enabled his dishonesty to go undetected, he would break with sin from that time forth.

But, Carey commented in a letter written to Andrew Fuller many years later, "a gracious God did not get me through."[12] Carey's dishonesty was discovered, and he was covered with shame and disgrace, afraid to even go abroad in the village for fear of what others were thinking. By this means, Carey was led, he subsequently said, "to see much more of myself than I had ever done before, and to seek for mercy with greater earnestness."[13] That mercy he found, as over the next two years he came to "depend on a crucified Saviour for pardon and salvation, and to seek a system of doctrines in the Word of God."[14]

BEFRIENDED BY CHATER AND SCOTT, AND MARRIAGE TO DOROTHY

William Carey continued to go with John Warr to the prayer meetings in Hackleton, but it was not until February 10,

---

12 Carey, *Memoir of William Carey*, 12.

13 Carey, *Memoir of William Carey*, 12.

14 Carey, *Memoir of William Carey*, 14.

1779, that he actually attended a worship service. On that day, a man named Thomas Chater (d. 1811), a resident of Olney, was preaching. The text on which Chater was preaching has not been recorded, but in his sermon he did quote that powerful exhortation in Hebrews 13:13: "Let us go forth therefore unto him [i.e., Jesus] without the camp, bearing his reproach." On the basis of this verse, Chater urged upon his hearers "the necessity of following Christ entirely." As Carey listened to Chater's exhortation, the interpretation that he made of this text and Chater's words was one that he would later describe as "very crude." He distinctly felt that God was calling him to leave the Church of England, where, in his particular parish church, he was sitting under "a lifeless, carnal ministry," and to unite with a Dissenting congregation. Since the Church of England was established by the law of the land, he reasoned, its members were "protected from the scandal of the cross."[15] So Carey became what he had long despised—a Dissenter.

When the Congregationalists in Hackleton decided to form themselves into a church on May 19, 1781, Carey was among the founders of what would eventually become Hackleton Baptist Church. Three weeks later, on Saturday, June 10, he married Dorothy Plackett (1756–1807), the illiterate daughter of a key member of the Hackleton congregation and a woman whose life has more often than not been misunderstood in the telling of Carey's story.[16] For the first four years of their married

---

15 Carey, *Memoir of William Carey*, 12.

16 By far, the best book on Dorothy Carey is that by James R. Beck, *Dorothy Carey: The*

life, William and Dorothy lived in Hackleton, where Carey had begun to preach in the Hackleton church.

During the summer of 1782, Chater befriended Carey by encouraging the Baptists in Earls Barton, a village six miles' walk from Hackleton, to ask Carey to preach in their meetinghouse, which has been described as "a paltry thatched cottage." Though the believers there could not pay him enough even to replace the shoes that he wore out in walking back and forth between Hackleton and Earls Barton, this one visit led to his preaching there once every fortnight for the next three and a half years.[17]

In this early period of his Christian life, Carey was also deeply helped by the preaching and friendship of the Anglican minister Thomas Scott, who had succeeded Newton as the minister in Olney. Though Carey heard Scott preach but a few times, he wrote to Ryland many years later, "If there be anything of the work of God in my soul, I owe much of it to Mr. Scott's preaching." Scott had a relative living in Hackleton, whom he often used to visit when he undertook itinerant preaching excursions. Somehow, he and Carey were introduced, and the latter took every opportunity to meet with him and ply him with questions. Carey never forgot the enormous help Scott was to him during these days. As he wrote in 1823, "I had frequent opportunities of conversation with him on subjects which to me were at that time of very great

Tragic and Untold Story of Mrs. William Carey (Grand Rapids, Mich.: Baker, 1992).

17   Carey, *William Carey*, 40–41.

importance, and frequently received hints or observations from him, which I remember with gratitude until to-day."[18]

JOHN SUTCLIFF AND ANDREW FULLER

It was in the summer of 1782 when Carey first preached in Earls Barton that he also first set eyes on John Sutcliff and Andrew Fuller. The annual assembly of the Northamptonshire Baptist Association, a group of sixteen or so Particular Baptist churches that spanned a number of English counties, was at Olney in Buckinghamshire in 1782, a market town where Sutcliff had been the pastor since 1775.[19] Sutcliff had come to faith in Christ in West Yorkshire, where he had sat under the preaching of John Fawcett (1740–1817), minister of Wainsgate Particular Baptist Church, who had been deeply affected by George Whitefield (1714–70) and William Grimshaw (1708–63).[20] After two years under Fawcett's mentorship, Sutcliff was driven by a hunger for further academic study to Bristol Baptist Academy in January 1772. Under the tutelage of Hugh Evans (1713–81), the principal of the

18 Carey, *William Carey*, 36; John Scott, *The Life of the Rev. Thomas Scott*, 8th ed. (London: L.B. Seeley and Son, 1825), 178–79.

19 For the life of Sutcliff, see Michael A. G. Haykin, *One Heart and One Soul: John Sutcliff of Olney, His Friends, and His Times* (Darlington, England: Evangelical, 1994). On the Northamptonshire Association, see Haykin, *One Heart and One Soul*, 110–13.

20 On Fawcett, see Michael A.G. Haykin, *"Blest Be the Tie That Binds": Remembering John Fawcett—His Times, His Life, His Hymn* (Louisville, Ky.: The Andrew Fuller Center for Baptist Studies, 2017).

academy, and his son Caleb (1737–91), Sutcliff had an outstanding academic record. He finished his studies at Bristol in May 1774, and, after brief preaching stints in Shrewsbury and Birmingham, he entered upon what would be his life's ministry in July 1775 at the Particular Baptist church in Olney. This market town was a veritable gospel center: John Newton had been the Anglican curate in the town from 1764 to 1779, when he had moved to London, and many in the town and surrounding countryside had come to faith under his preaching. Moreover, the great evangelical poet and hymn writer William Cowper (1731–1800), who had been a close friend of Newton, still resided in the town in his three-story red-brick house in the southeast corner of the marketplace, right across from the Baptist church.[21] Sutcliff pastored in Olney for thirty-nine years. This lengthy ministry built up the Baptist work there and encouraged other churches in neighboring towns and villages, and Sutcliff came to acquire a justly deserved reputation for "sound judgment and warm affection" for Christ, His cause, and His people.[22]

Andrew Fuller, unlike Sutcliff, had no formal theological education, but, like Carey, his social background was that of the lower classes. In fact, the evangelical statesman William Wilberforce (1759–1833), who deeply appreciated Fuller's

---

21 Cowper's home is now the Cowper & Newton Museum (http://www.cowperand-newtonmuseum.org.uk).

22 The quote comes from Christopher Anderson, letter to Andrew Fuller, July 7, 1814, in Hugh Anderson, *The Life and Letters of Christopher Anderson* (Edinburgh, Scotland: William P. Kennedy, 1854), 224.

theological acumen, once told his sons that Fuller was "the very picture of a blacksmith."[23] Fuller was born in Wicken, a small agricultural village in Cambridgeshire, in 1754.[24] His parents, Robert Fuller (1723–81) and Philippa Gunton (1726–1816), were farmers who rented a succession of dairy farms. In 1761, his parents moved a short distance to Soham, where he and his family began to regularly attend the local Particular Baptist church, and where Fuller was converted in November 1769. After being baptized the following spring, he became a member of the Soham church. In 1774, Fuller was called to the pastorate of this work. He stayed until 1782, when he became the pastor of the Particular Baptist congregation at Kettering.

Fuller's time as a pastor in Soham was a decisive period for the shaping of Fuller's theological perspective. It was during this period that he began a lifelong study of the works of the American divine Jonathan Edwards (1703–58), whom Miklós Vetö has described rightly as "the greatest Christian theologian of the eighteenth century."[25] Fuller's close reading of Edwards' writings, along with his commitment to live under the authority of

---

23 Robert Isaac Wilberforce and Samuel Wilberforce, *The Life of William Wilberforce* (London: John Murray, 1839), III:388–89.

24 For Fuller's life, the classic study is that of John Ryland, *The Work of Faith, the Labour of Love, and the Patience of Hope Illustrated; in the Life and Death of the Reverend Andrew Fuller* (London: Button & Son, 1816). A second edition of this biography appeared in 1818. For more recent studies, see Paul Brewster, *Andrew Fuller: Model Pastor-Theologian*, Studies in Baptist Life and Thought (Nashville, Tenn.: B&H, 2010), and Peter J. Morden, *The Life and Thought of Andrew Fuller (1754–1815)*, Studies in Evangelical History and Thought (Milton Keynes, England: Paternoster, 2015).

25 Miklós Vetö, "Book Reviews: *America's Theologian: A Recommendation of Jonathan Edwards.* By Robert W. Jenson," *Church History* 58 (1989): 522.

the infallible Scriptures, enabled him to become what his close friend John Ryland Jr. described as "perhaps the most judicious and able theological writer that ever belonged to our denomination."[26] Succeeding generations have confirmed Ryland's estimation of his friend. C.H. Spurgeon (1834–92), for instance, once described Fuller as the "greatest theologian" of his century, while A.C. Underwood, a twentieth-century Baptist historian, said of Fuller—in a statement that clearly echoes Ryland's estimation—that "he was the soundest and most creatively useful theologian the Particular Baptists have ever had."[27]

The friendship of Fuller was particularly important to Carey: Fuller was his chief supporter in England, and Fuller's theology lay at the heart of Carey's missionary vision.

SEEING GUY AND FULLER

Carey, used to walking considerable distances, tramped over to Olney from his home in the early hours of Wednesday, June 5. A huge crowd had turned up to the Baptist meetinghouse in Olney that morning—so large, in fact, there were not enough seats in the building. The weather being nice, seats were set up in the yard behind the church, and the preachers stood in one of the windowsills, the window having been removed, so those

---

26 John Ryland, *The Indwelling and Righteousness of Christ No Security against Corporeal Death, but the Source of Spiritual and Eternal Life* (London, 1815), 2–3.

27 The Spurgeon remark is taken from Gilbert Laws, *Andrew Fuller: Pastor, Theologian, Ropeholder* (London: Carey, 1942), 127; A.C. Underwood, *A History of the English Baptists* (London: The Baptist Union Publication Dept. [Kingsgate Press], 1947), 166.

inside the church building as well as those in the churchyard could hear them. We do not know where Carey was seated that evening as he listened to Fuller's robust sermon on 1 Corinthians 14:20 ("Brethren, be not children in understanding: howbeit in malice be ye children, but in understanding be men"). But it had been a spiritual feast all day, for in the morning he had heard William Guy (1739–83) preach a powerful sermon on 2 Peter 3:18.[28] John Ryland Jr. once described Guy as "the plainest rough-hewed you ever saw or heard," but God had powerfully employed his preaching in a significant revival in his church in Shepshed, Leicestershire, in the mid-1770s, when some worship services had gone on for up to eight hours.

With regard to Fuller's preaching, we are told that he was not "the exact model of an orator" and had "none of that eloquence which consists in a felicitous selection of terms." Nonetheless, his presence in the pulpit was imposing and solemn, "tending to inspire awe," and his delivery was marked by boldness and a "great force of expression." He would be "deeply impressed with his subject, and anxious to produce a similar impression on his hearers." Few who heard him did so without satisfaction—"if the heart were not at all times affected, yet the judgment would be informed."[29] Carey long

---

28 "Breviates" in Andrew Fuller, *The Excellence and Utility of the Grace of Hope* (Northampton, England: T. Dicey and Co., 1782), 13.

29 J.W. Morris, *Memoirs of the Life and Writings of the Rev. Andrew Fuller* (London, 1816), 66–68. See also the helpful essay by Keith S. Grant, "Plain, Evangelical, and Affectionate: The Preaching of Andrew Fuller (1754–1815)," *Crux* 48, no. 1 (Spring 2012): 12–22.

remembered the sermons of Guy and Fuller, as well as the fact that he fasted the entire day because he had no money to purchase a noonday meal. All through his years at Hackleton, Carey labored at the trade for which he had been trained, but his shoemaking provided only the slenderest of incomes, and certainly left nothing for eating out.[30]

Carey had been helped in his early Christian life by the friendship of strong Christians including John Warr, Thomas Chater, and Thomas Scott. Carey's relationships with these men were relatively short lived. But, by his own testimony, the impact they had on him was long lasting. Warr's witness was vitally used by God to bring him to Christ. Chater helped him see that he had to follow Christ wholeheartedly, which, to Carey's mind at the time, meant leaving the Anglican state church and joining a small Dissenting village cause. Obviously, this did not prejudice Carey against Anglicans, since he later enjoyed the friendship of the Anglican rector Thomas Scott. These small friendships are a good reminder that God uses seemingly minor relationships to accomplish great things. But, as we shall see in the next chapter, it was especially his lifelong friendships with Sutcliff, Fuller, and Ryland that would be decisive for the transformative nature of his Christian pilgrimage.

---

30 Carey, *Memoir of William Carey*, 15–16.

CHAPTER TWO

Good Friendships: A Road to Theological Maturity

During the first few years after his conversion, William Carey's "mind was much employed in obtaining just and scriptural sentiments," as his friend Andrew Fuller once put it.[1] Carey himself later spoke of his early days as a Christian: "Having so slight an acquaintance with ministers, I was obliged to draw all from the Bible alone."[2] Yet, as we have seen, Carey did have an early friendship with Thomas Scott that was enormously helpful to him. And being exposed to

---

1 Andrew Fuller, "Attempt at collecting some particulars of the life of Dr. Carey," Fuller Baptist Church, Kettering, 3. This little-known manuscript by Fuller is the earliest biographical sketch of Carey. It can be found in its entirety in Eustace Carey, *Memoir of William Carey, D.D.* (London: Jackson and Walford, 1836), 67–78.

2 Carey, *Memoir of William Carey*, 16.

the solid preaching of men such as Fuller and William Guy would also have been immensely important. As Carey studied the Scriptures, he became convinced that believer's baptism was the biblical model for this ordinance. So, in 1783, he approached John Ryland Sr. (1723–92), pastor of College Lane Baptist Church in Northampton, for baptism.

Carey had first seen the elder Ryland the previous June when he went to the association meeting at Olney; Ryland had opened the evening service in prayer.[3] Like Fuller, he was an imposing figure in the pulpit. But unlike Fuller, he was quite an eccentric figure, an important fact that will come up later in this chapter. Ryland first gave young Carey a pamphlet on baptism and then asked his son, John Ryland Jr., to baptize the young cobbler.

The younger Ryland was copastor with his father of the College Lane cause.[4] When his father moved to Enfield, near London, in 1786, Ryland became the sole pastor. During his early ministerial experience, Ryland, like Fuller, read deeply in the writings of Jonathan Edwards. Indeed, after the Scriptures, Edwards' writings exerted the strongest theological influence

---

3   "Breviates" in Andrew Fuller, *The Excellence and Utility of the Grace of Hope* (Northampton, England: T. Dicey and Co., 1782), 13.

4   On Ryland's life and thought, see L.G. Champion, "The Theology of John Ryland: Its Sources and Influences," *The Baptist Quarterly* 28 (1979–80): 17–18, 26; Michael A.G. Haykin, "John Ryland, Jr.—'O Lord, I Would Delight in Thee': The Life and Ministry of John Ryland, Jr. Appreciated on the 250th Anniversary of His Birth," *Reformation Today* 196 (November–December 2003): 13–20; Chris Crocker, "The Life and Legacy of John Ryland Jr. (1753–1825): A Man of Considerable Usefulness—An Historical Biography" (Ph.D. thesis, Bristol Baptist College, 2018).

on Carey, Ryland, Fuller, and their friends. In particular, the works of Edwards helped this circle of brothers see how classical Calvinism could speak to the men and women of the late eighteenth and early nineteenth centuries, and they also stimulated a hunger for corporate revival, personal renewal, and mission. These three aspects of Edwards' theological reflection provided both shape and substance for the theology of these friends. As C.H. Spurgeon once remarked about the thinking of Carey:

> Carey was the living model of [Jonathan] Edwards' theology, or rather of pure Christianity. His was not a theology which left out the backbone and strength of religion—not a theology, on the other hand, all bones and skeleton, a lifeless thing without a soul: his theology was full-orbed Calvinism, high as you please, but practical godliness so low that many called it legal.[5]

So, in the early hours of October 5, 1785, the younger Ryland immersed Carey in the River Nene that then flowed through Northampton. Obviously, at the time, neither of these two men realized what the future would hold, and how they would become firm friends and co-laborers in a great work of God.

---

5   "C.H. Spurgeon's Tribute to William Carey," *The Baptist Times*, Supplement (April 16, 1992): 1.

A GROWING PASSION FOR MISSIONS

Around the time of his baptism, Carey came across the accounts of the three voyages of discovery undertaken by the superb maritime navigator James Cook in the Pacific from 1768 to 1779, which involved, among other things, the discovery of Tahiti and the charting of the unknown shores of New Zealand and Australia. Iain H. Murray has rightly observed that "the end of Cook's geographical feat [was] the beginning of missionary enterprise."[6] Carey would later say regarding his perusal of these volumes, "Reading Cook's voyages was the first thing that engaged my mind to think of missions."[7] Through these accounts, Carey's boyhood desire to know about other lands was given substance and shape. More importantly, through the written account of Cook's voyages, Carey began to gaze upon wider spiritual horizons than the fields of Northamptonshire and to reflect on the desperate spiritual plight of those who lived in the countries that Cook had discovered. Many of them had no written language, certainly none of them had the Scriptures in their own tongues, and there were neither local churches nor resident ministers to share the good news of God's salvation. "Pity, therefore, humanity, and much more Christianity," he wrote only a few years after reading Cook's journals, calling "loudly for every

---

6   Iain H. Murray, "Divine Providence and Captain Cook," *The Banner of Truth* 274 (July 1986): 7.

7   Carey, *Memoir of William Carey*, 18.

possible exertion to introduce the gospel amongst them."[8] Over the next eight years, one of his main preoccupations was the collection of information, especially geographical and religious, about these nations, including the many other nations of the world that had never heard a word of the gospel.

Carey's growing passion for the evangelization of nations outside Europe did not cause him to forget the need of the many at his own back door. Through his witness, for example, his two sisters, Mary and Ann, were won to Christ by 1783. As is often the case with the members of one's own family, William had not found it at all easy to speak to them concerning their need of Christ. But he persevered in praying for them, and when Mary Carey thought back on this period of her life, she could only exclaim, "O what a privilege to have praying relations, and what a mercy to have a God that waits to be gracious!"[9]

By the time that his sisters were converted, William Carey had begun preaching. He first preached at the Congregationalist church in Hackleton. In 1785, he became a member of John Sutcliff's Olney church and had the opportunity to preach there on July 14 of that year. Thirteen months later, on the evening of August 10, 1786, he was formally ordained to the ministry of the gospel, and, in the words of the Olney Church minute book, he was "sent out by the Church to

---

8 William Carey, *An Enquiry into the Obligations of Christians, to Use Means for the Conversion of the Heathens* (1792; repr. London: Baptist Missionary Society, 1934), 13.

9 Carey, *Memoir of William Carey*, 32–33.

preach the Gospel, wherever God in his providence might call him."[10]

By this time, he and Dorothy were living in a village called Moulton, Northamptonshire, a few miles to the northeast of Northampton. Carey became involved with the Moulton church, a General (that is, Arminian) Baptist work, and asked Sutcliff for help in drawing up a covenant for the church.[11] As he informed Sutcliff:

> It will be easy to settle the church upon evangelical principles, but I do not choose to attempt such a thing without your advice and concurrence. If you approve of it, I should be glad if you would send me word, and likewise the outlines of a covenant, which if strict in practical, and not too high in doctrinal points, will, I believe, be unanimously subscribed by all the old members of the church. . . . The friends are desirous to be in order. . . .[12]

---

10 "Extracts from the Olney Church Book" in John Taylor, ed., *Biographical and Literary Notices of William Carey, D.D.* (Northampton, England: Dryden, Taylor & Son/London: Alexander & Shepheard, 1886), 2.

11 The Moulton church, now called Carey Baptist Church, as well as the cottage in which William and Dorothy lived, can still be seen at the west end of West Street in the village today. For the church, see http://www.careybaptist.org.uk/default.php. The Moulton Baptist witness goes back into the seventeenth century. See also "The Carey Experience" (http://www.thecareyexperience.co.uk/index.htm), a tour of five sites in Northamptonshire and North Buckinghamshire relating to Carey.

12 William Carey, Letter to John Sutcliff, December 30, 1785, in Taylor, *Biographical and Literary Notices*, 36.

A good number of seventeenth- and eighteenth-century British churches sought to promote and safeguard their experience as communities of Christian disciples by the adoption of a written covenant. The heart of these church covenants was usually a series of carefully formulated commitments that were biblically based and that church members voluntarily made to God and to one another. Whereas confessions of faith are centered mainly on vital doctrinal issues, these covenants dealt primarily with Christian conduct.

Sutcliff appears to have sent Carey "the outlines of a covenant" that became the basis for the one signed by the members of the Moulton church on Sunday, October 1, 1786. The following month, Carey assumed his first pastorate as he accepted the call of the Baptist church to become their pastor.[13] Carey's salary from the church, though, was so small that he had to supplement his income with monies derived from shoemaking and teaching.

FORMING LIFELONG FRIENDSHIPS

Carey's formal ordination to the pastorate of the Moulton church took place on Wednesday, August 1, 1787. Taking part in his ordination that day were three Baptist pastors—all of whom we have already met—who would become lifelong friends and who would be the pillars of the Baptist Missionary

---

13 "Extracts from the Moulton Church Book" in Taylor, *Biographical and Literary Notices*, 2.

Society (BMS) that sent Carey to India: John Ryland Jr., Andrew Fuller, and John Sutcliff. As we have noted, it is quite misleading to suppose that it was Carey's singlehanded effort that brought about the founding of the BMS and enabled him to accomplish all that he did in India from 1793 till his death more than forty years later. Carey was part of this close-knit circle of like-minded friends, without whom little of what he longed for would have been realized. The Scottish Baptist preacher Christopher Anderson, who was well acquainted with a number of Carey's close friends, maintained during Carey's lifetime that it was the "strong personal attachment" of these friends to one another that lay behind the "usefulness" of the BMS.[14]

At the ordination service, after Carey had presented his statement of faith, Ryland asked him various questions about his theological convictions. Ryland noted in his diary that Carey's theological convictions were "sound and sensible."[15] Sutcliff then gave a charge to Carey from 2 Timothy 4:5 that, regrettably, has not survived.[16] In fact, only one of Sutcliff's sermons has been transmitted, and we shall look at it later in this chapter. We do have a detailed outline of Fuller's sermon, though, which he addressed to the Moulton church.

---

14 Christopher Anderson, *The Christian Spirit Which Is Essential to the Triumph of the Kingdom of God* (London, 1824), 22–27.

15 "Extracts from the Diary of the Late Rev. Dr. Ryland" in Taylor, *Biographical and Literary Notices*, 34.

16 "Extracts from the Moulton Church Book" in Taylor, *Biographical and Literary Notices*, 3, and "Extracts from the Diary of the Late Rev. Dr. Ryland" in Taylor, *Biographical and Literary Notices*, 34.

Based on Psalm 68:18, the verse that Paul cites in Ephesians 4 regarding the gifts of the ascended Christ to the church, Fuller first noted that Christian ministers are a great blessing for God's people. As gifts from God, ministers are "designed to supply Christ's absence in a sort" as well as being shepherds for God's flock. Moreover, Christ gave His life to secure the gift of these pastors. Fuller thus admonished the Moulton congregation: "Make much of the gift [of Carey as their pastor] on this account."[17] Why has God given such gifts to the church through Christ? For an answer, Fuller turned to the last clause of Psalm 68:18, "that the Lord God might dwell among them," that is, His people:

> "Will God indeed dwell with men?" He will; and how? It is by the means of ordinances and ministers. A church of Christ is God's house, and where any one builds a house it is a token that he means to dwell there. What a blessing to a village, a country, for God to build a house in it. It is by this that we may hope for a blessing upon the means to the conversion of our children and friends, and for the edification of believers.[18]

---

17 Andrew Fuller, "Importance of Christian Ministers Considered as the Gift of Christ" in *The Complete Works of the Rev. Andrew Fuller* (1845; repr. Harrisonburg, Va.: Sprinkle, 1988), 1:521–22.

18 Fuller, "Importance of Christian Ministers" in *Complete Works of the Rev. Andrew Fuller*, 1:522.

Fuller well knew that all ministers are but men, and "as men, and as sinful men, ministers are as nothing."[19] But as gifts to the church, they are one of the key means by which God inhabits His church and blesses His people. This really is a remarkable statement and bespeaks a very high view of vocational ministry. Through the ministry of pastors, especially their preaching, God will bring the children and friends of the members of the congregation to saving faith and will also build them up.

CAREY REBUKED[20]

Carey's pastorate at Moulton admitted him to meeting periodically with other Baptist ministers who pastored churches in the Northamptonshire Baptist Association. This association provided both pastors and laity with a forum for the exchange of ideas, a meeting place for fellowship as well as for mutual spiritual encouragement. At a meeting of the pastors of this association on September 30, 1785, one of the senior pastors of the group, John Ryland Sr.—whom, as we have seen, Carey had approached regarding baptism—is said to have asked Carey and another young pastor, John Webster

---

19 Fuller, "Importance of Christian Ministers" in *Complete Works of the Rev. Andrew Fuller*, 1:521.

20 For what follows in this section, see Michael A.G. Haykin, *One Heart and One Soul: John Sutcliff of Olney, His Friends, and His Times* (Darlington, England: Evangelical, 1994), 193–96. See also the discussion of this event by Brian Stanley, *The History of the Baptist Missionary Society 1792–1992* (Edinburgh, Scotland: T&T Clark, 1992), 6–7.

Morris (1763–1836), pastor of Clipston Baptist Church in Northamptonshire, to offer those gathered that day some topics for conversation. Carey suggested a question that had been running through his mind for some time: "Whether the command given to the apostles to teach all nations was not binding on all succeeding ministers, to the end of the world, seeing that the accompanying promise was of equal extent." Carey's question obviously grew out of meditation upon Matthew 28:18–20. If, Carey reasoned, Christ's promise of His presence with His people is for all time (v. 20), what then of His command to "teach all nations" about Christ (v. 19)? Is it not a requirement for the church till the end of history as we know it?

According to Morris, Ryland responded with some vehemence to Carey's suggestion and bluntly called the young pastor "a most miserable enthusiast," that is, a total fanatic, for asking such a question. The senior minister went on:

Nothing could be done before another Pentecost, when an effusion of miraculous gifts, including the gift of tongues, would give effect to the commission of Christ as at first. . . . What, sir, can you preach in Arabic, in Persic, in Hindustani, in Bengali, sir; that you think it our duty to send the gospel to the heathen?[21]

---

21   J.W. Morris, *Memoirs of the Life and Writings of the Rev. Andrew Fuller* (London,

John C. Marshman (1794–1877), the son of Carey's coworker in India, Joshua Marshman, had a similar report about the words of the elder Ryland. As Marshman reported the incident many years later in 1859, Ryland apparently dismissed the proposed topic with a frown and told Carey: "Young man, sit down. When God pleases to convert the heathen, he will do it without your aid or mine!"[22] On the other hand, John Ryland Jr. strongly asserted that his father never uttered such sentiments.[23] The preponderance of evidence, however, does seem to indicate that Carey did indeed receive some sort of stinging rebuke from the elder Ryland.

CONTENDING WITH HYPER-CALVINISM

The standard interpretation of the elder Ryland's reasoning traces it back to the influence of hyper-Calvinism.[24] This seems to be doubtful as an adequate theological explanation of Ryland's outburst. Rather, it probably had to do with his view

---

1816), 96–97; J.W. Morris, *Memoirs of the Life and Writings of the Rev. Andrew Fuller*, 2nd ed. (London: Wightman and Cramp, 1826), 100, 100n*.

22 John Clark Marshman, *The Life and Times of Carey, Marshman, and Ward* (1859; repr., Serampore, India: Council of Serampore College, 2005), 1:10.

23 Ryland, *The Life and Death of the Rev. Andrew Fuller*, 112n*.

24 See, for example, F. Deaville Walker, *William Carey: Missionary Pioneer and Statesman* (1925; repr. Chicago: Moody Press, n.d.), 55, who attributes Ryland's remarks to "ultra-Calvinistic theories"; Timothy George, *Faithful Witness: The Life and Mission of William Carey* (Birmingham, Ala.: New Hope, 1991), 54–55; Malcolm B. Yarnell III, *The Heart of a Baptist* (White Paper, No. 2; Fort Worth, Tex.: The Center for Theological Research, Southwestern Baptist Theological Seminary, 2005), 2–3.

of the timing of various future events. Ryland had adopted the end-times thinking of John Gill (1697–1771), the leading Baptist theologian of his day, in which the gospel could not be taken unhindered to the nations till the two witnesses of Revelation 11 were slain, something that would not happen till well into the nineteenth century.[25] Wrong thinking, yes, but the elder Ryland is not the hyper-Calvinist bogeyman of far too many treatments of Baptist history.[26]

However, there is little doubt that hyper-Calvinism was a major challenge with which Carey and his circle of Baptist friends had to contend. Hyper-Calvinists in this period maintained that because the unsaved could not respond to the call of Christ in the preaching of the gospel without the enablement of God, then it was not their responsibility to repent and believe, and consequently, pastors had no duty to exhort the lost to come to Christ.

Carey's close friend Andrew Fuller had handily refuted this error in his tremendous exegetical study *The Gospel Worthy of All Acceptation*, which first appeared in 1785 (a second edition was issued in 1801). In this work, Fuller demonstrates from the Scriptures that it is the duty of sinners to believe the gospel even though the power to believe is entirely dependent on God's grace. He also shows that the gospel must be freely offered to sinners far and wide.

---

25 See Carey, *Enquiry into the Obligations of Christians*, 12, where Carey ascribes this view to "some learned divines."

26 See Iain H. Murray, "William Carey: Climbing the Rainbow," *The Banner of Truth* 349 (October 1992): 20–21.

Carey took Fuller's theology in this regard as his own starting point. Further, in his own written defense of crosscultural missions, *An Enquiry into the Obligations of Christians, to Use Means for the Conversion of the Heathens* (1792), he noted that some of his contemporaries had argued that the command to make disciples from all the nations was no longer binding upon the church. The ancient church, they maintained, had actually fulfilled that command. Moreover, according to Carey, they argued thus: "We have enough to do to attend to the salvation of our own countrymen; and that, if God intends the salvation of the heathen, he will some way or other bring them to the gospel, or the gospel to them."[27] Carey was able to refute this argument by pointing out that the two other aspects of the text in Matthew 28—baptism and the presence of Christ—had no temporal limitations on them. The command to baptize was still very much in force, and the promise of Christ's abiding presence was still a comfort in time of trouble and turmoil.[28]

Carey . . . an Arminian?

Given this theological atmosphere, it is not surprising that people could react to Carey in a manner described by the younger John Ryland. This description comes from Ryland's diary entry for July 8, 1788:

---

27 Carey, *Enquiry into the Obligations of Christians*, 8.

28 Carey, *Enquiry into the Obligations of Christians*, 8–9.

Asked Brother Carey to preach. Some of our people who are wise above what is written, would not hear him, called him an Arminian, and discovered a strange spirit. Lord pity us! I am almost worn out with grief at these foolish cavils against some of the best of my brethren, men of God, who are only hated because of their zeal.[29]

Carey was a Calvinist, but an evangelical one, of the same ilk as John Bunyan (1628–88), the powerful preacher of the previous century; Jonathan Edwards, the great New England theologian of revival; and George Whitefield, the leading evangelist of the eighteenth century. In his theology, Carey married a deep-seated conviction regarding God's sovereignty in salvation to an equally profound belief that in converting sinners God uses means.[30]

Now, what is striking with regard to so much of the literature about William Carey is that it is decidedly atheological, as if Carey's theology was of little importance to his missionary zeal and achievement. However, as Iain H. Murray has written regarding biographical studies: "Biographies show that doctrinal belief is not a secondary or theoretical thing; rather, it has vital consequence in the way Christians live. Weak doctrine

---

29 Cited in A. de M. Chesterman, "The Journals of David Brainerd and of William Carey," *The Baptist Quarterly* 19 (1961–62): 151–52.

30 David Kingdon, "William Carey and the Origins of the Modern Missionary Movement," in *Fulfilling the Great Commission* (London: The Westminster Conference, 1992), 88.

produces weak lives. Those who 'turn the world upside down' are always those 'mighty in the Scriptures.'"[31] If Murray is right, then, when we ask what made William Carey and we fail to refer to his doctrinal convictions, we fail to read Carey's life correctly. To put it plainly: without understanding Carey's consistent delight in Calvinism throughout his life, we cannot understand the man, his motivation, or eventually the shape of his mission. One of the best places to see this delight is in what is called the Leicester Covenant.

THE WITNESS OF THE LEICESTER COVENANT

In April 1789, Carey informed his Moulton congregation that he had received an invitation to become the pastor of Harvey Lane Baptist Church in Leicester. General Baptists had been in Leicester since the late 1640s, but Harvey Lane, a Particular Baptist congregation, dated from 1760.[32] After much prayer by the Careys and the Moulton congregation, William and Dorothy concluded that the Lord was leading them to Leicester, and moved there in the summer of 1789. The Harvey Lane church, though, was weak and dispirited, and some of its members were leading openly dissolute lives. One of the latter was the previous pastor, John Blackshaw, who preached his final sermon in June 1788, but was disfellowshiped the

---

31 Iain H. Murray, "A Revival of Calvinism," *Tabletalk* 35, no. 8 (August 2011): 78.

32 Sheila Mitchell, *Not Disobedient . . . A History of United Baptist Church, Leicester including Harvey Lane 1760–1845, Belvoir Street 1845–1940 and Charles Street 1831–1940* ([Leicester], 1984), 16–17.

following year for being "frequently intoxicated with liquor."[33] The members were divided over what to do to restore the work, so Carey took the radical step of dissolving the church in 1790 and reforming it on the basis of a covenant.

The covenant that Carey used to reorganize the church, known as the Leicester Covenant, was based in part on the church's original 1760 covenant.[34] Most of the covenant, as was typical of such documents in Baptist circles, dealt with issues of practice and behavior. But in the second article, Carey laid out the theological convictions upon which membership in the church was based:

> We receive the Bible as the Word of God, and the only rule of faith, and practice, in which we find the following doctrines taught, namely, that in the Deity are three equal persons, the Father, the Son, and the Holy Spirit, who sustain distinct offices in the economy of human salvation; We believe that all things were fully known to God from the foundation of the world, that he from eternity chose his people in Christ to salvation through sanctification of the Spirit and belief of the truth; that all rational creatures are under indispensable obligation to obey the Law of God, which is holy, just and good, but that all men have broken it and are liable to eternal punishment; that

---

33 Mitchell, *Not Disobedient . . . A History of United Baptist Church, Leicester*, 20.
34 Mitchell, *Not Disobedient . . . A History of United Baptist Church, Leicester*, 25.

in the fullness of time God sent his Son to redeem his people whose blood was a sufficient atonement for sin, and by the imputation of whose righteousness we are accounted righteous before God, and accepted with him; and that being justified by faith we have peace with God through our Lord Jesus Christ. We further believe that men are totally depraved, and that the carnal mind is enmity against God, and that we are convicted, and converted only by the sovereign operations of the Holy Spirit upon our hearts, being made willing in the day of his power, and that the life of grace is maintained by the same divine Spirit, who is the finisher as well as the author of our faith, that those who are received thus shall persevere in the way of holiness, and at last obtain everlasting happiness through the mercy of God.[35]

In addition to the standard evangelical convictions about the authority of the Scriptures and the classical doctrine of the Trinity, Carey also affirmed here God's sovereign election of a people whom He saved by His Son's atoning work and justified by the imputation of His Son's righteous, flawless life. This work of grace was needed due to the radical depravity

---

35 From John Appleby, *"I Can Plod . . ." William Carey and the Early Years of the First Baptist Missionary Society* (London: Grace, 2007), 285. Carey, in turn, transcribed it from a photocopy of the original church minute book held in the Record Office for Leicestershire, Leicester, and Rutland, Wigston Magna, Leicester. For the full covenant, see Appendix 2.

of all mankind, for this pattern of wrongdoing and sin was so deeply embedded in the human heart and made human beings so hostile to God that only the unconquerable work of the Spirit could overcome it. As Carey noted in another context, one "may well expect to see fire and water agree, as persons with sinful hearts and desires cordially approve of the character of God."[36] Again, the Baptist leader later commented that he took great comfort from the fact that "divine power can subdue all things; and without the Holy Spirit, nothing effectual can be done anywhere, or under any circumstances."[37] This work of the Spirit, Carey later affirmed, was rooted in the fact that Christ "died in the stead of sinners. We deserved the wrath of God; but he endured it. We could make no sufficient atonement for our guilt; but he completely made an end of sin."[38]

Once this people have been converted, Carey went on to affirm in the Leicester Covenant, the all-divine Holy Spirit will keep them loyal to Christ to the end, when they shall "obtain everlasting happiness through the mercy of God." It is noteworthy that Carey himself was later certain that those "proofs I have of the evil tendency of my heart . . . convince me that I need the constant influence of the Holy Spirit; and that, if God did not continue his loving-kindness to me, I

---

36 Cited in Carey, *Memoir of William Carey*, 418.

37 William Carey, Letter to Samuel Pearce, January 29, [1795], in *Periodical Accounts relative to the Baptist Missionary Society* (Clipston, England: J.W. Morris, 1800), I:127.

38 Cited in Carey, *Memoir of William Carey*, 418–19.

should as certainly depart from him, and become an open profligate, as I exist."[39]

TAKING STOCK

Between 1783 and 1789, Carey made three significant friendships: with John Sutcliff, who was his pastor for a period of time during these years; with Andrew Fuller, who may well have been his closest friend in the years that followed; and with John Ryland Jr., who baptized him as a believer. These friendships helped Carey mature as a Christian and brought to bear on his life a treasured tradition of Christian literature, especially the writings of the American divine Jonathan Edwards. Thus, when Carey sailed to India, among the few books he took with him was a volume of Edwards' sermons.[40] Carey's Leicester Covenant is an excellent vantage point from which to gauge the theological impact that these friendships and literature had on Carey. In other ways, though, Carey was the leader among this band of brothers: the fire of his passion for global evangelization would soon envelop and enflame them, as we shall see in our next chapter.

---

39 Cited in Carey, *Memoir of William Carey*, 19–20. For this quote and the previous one, I am indebted to Andrew Kerr's work on Carey's adherence to the so-called Five Points of Calvinism, "The Botanist's Tulip: Calvinism in the Writings of William Carey" (Unpublished paper, March 2009, in possession of the author).

40 See, for example, Carey's diary entry for June 28, 1793, in Terry G. Carter, collected and ed., *The Journal and Selected Letters of William Carey* (Macon, Ga.: Smyth & Helwys, 2000), 4.

CHAPTER THREE

The Pathway
to Global Mission

The sole sermon of Carey's pastor, John Sutcliff, that has survived in a complete form was given at a meeting of the pastors of the Northamptonshire Association on April 27, 1791, in the Baptist church at Clipston, Northamptonshire, where John Webster Morris was the pastor.[1] Titled "Jealousy for the Lord of Hosts," Sutcliff's sermon was based on 1 Kings 19:10, in particular Elijah's statement, "I have been very jealous for the LORD, the God of hosts."[2]

---

1   A Baptist chapel at Clipston had been built in 1778, though there is evidence that there were Baptists in the village as far back as 1718. This was the building in which Fuller preached his sermon. In 1803, when Francis Augustus Cox was the minister, this first church building was entirely torn down, and its brick and other salvageable materials used in the construction of the present church building. The front facade is Victorian, and was added in 1861. See details in Alison Collier and Jeremy Thompson, *Clipston: A Heritage*, 2nd ed. (Leicester, England: Troubadour, 2009), 55–60. In Fuller's day, Clipston was spelled with a final *e*.

2   John Sutcliff and Andrew Fuller, *Jealousy for the Lord of Hosts: and, The Pernicious Influence of Delay in Religious Concerns. Two Discourses Delivered at a Meeting*

The subject of "divine jealousy" had long been on Sutcliff's mind. Ten years previously, on March 13, 1781, he had written a letter to Fuller in which he had expressed some of his thoughts on this subject and had told Fuller that to him it was "a source of many reflections."[3] The ministerial meeting in Clipston ten years later provided him with the perfect opportunity finally to gather together these reflections and share them with others. Fuller also preached on this occasion. It is vital to see that Carey's vision for global missions was not simply his, but by this time had come to be shared by his friends Sutcliff and Fuller. So, in this chapter, we shall look at these sermons in detail and see the way that Carey's close friends understood the mission of the church. We will then turn to examine Carey's quintessential plea for missions, *An Enquiry into the Obligations of Christians, to Use Means for the Conversion of the Heathens.* This tract appeared in 1792, the year after the Clipston sermons of his faithful friends Sutcliff and Fuller, which were key steps in Carey's path to mission in India.

SUTCLIFF'S SERMON

In "Jealousy for the Lord of Hosts," Sutcliff first drew a distinction between jealousy *for* and jealousy *of* an object. While

---

of *Ministers at Clipstone, in Northamptonshire, April 27, 1791* (London, 1791). Sutcliff's sermon is reproduced in Haykin, *One Heart and One Soul*, 355–65. Quotations from Sutcliff's sermon in the pages that follow are taken from the latter.

3   Andrew Fuller, letter to John Sutcliff, March 13, 1781, Letters of Andrew Fuller, typescript transcript, Angus Library, Regent's Park College, University of Oxford, England.

the latter is not at all a desirable sentiment, the former "implies love to and tender concern for" the object toward which it is directed. When Elijah therefore spoke of his being "very jealous for the LORD, the God of hosts," he was declaring that he was gripped by a love and concern for God's "honor and interest." Sutcliff then went on to detail three attitudes that are intimate companions of such jealousy for God: a reverent obedience to the Scriptures as an "infallible guide," "a spirit of universal benevolence," and a habitual concern for the cause of Christ. Particularly noteworthy are Sutcliff's remarks about the first and second of these attitudes. Sutcliff laid great stress on the vital importance of bringing the entirety of one's beliefs and life into conformity with the revealed will of God as found in the Scriptures. True jealousy for God is accompanied by unmitigated obedience to these ancient, yet ever new, texts. They are an "infallible guide" and "unerring rule," Sutcliff reminded his hearers, by means of which a believer can test the reality of his faith and the purity of his doctrine, experience, worship, and lifestyle. Sutcliff clearly regarded the Word of God as critical in transforming the lives and thoughts of sinful men and women. It is noteworthy that the English-speaking missionary movement began with men passionately committed to the authority and inerrancy of the Bible.

Genuine jealousy for God is conscious of the needs of others—all others, not merely one's own circle of friends and intimate associates. Drawing on Paul's words in 1 Corinthians 6:17, Sutcliff argued that Christians bear a resemblance to their Lord. Even as Christ shows benevolence to all of humanity, so "saints feel a similar temper." Their benevolence seeks the temporal and especially the eternal good of their neighbors. And, Sutcliff reminded his hearers, included among one's neighbors are not only those of "your own society, or those enclosed in the small circle of your personal acquaintance," but "every member of the human race," wherever they may be found. For such love and benevolence "can embrace a globe. It can stretch its arms like seas, and grasp in all the habitable shores." Given the way in which Sutcliff developed his understanding of "a spirit of universal benevolence" as an inseparable corollary of jealousy for God, it is not at all surprising that, as he sought to apply his remarks to his hearers' lives, he focused on prayer and evangelism. Those who are jealous for God and who consequently possess "a spirit of universal benevolence" should give themselves to "fervent prayer for the outpouring of the divine Spirit" that they might "see the advancement of the Redeemer's kingdom." Without the empowering of the Spirit of God, "the greatest human abilities labor in vain, and the noblest efforts fail of success."

This deep reliance on the Holy Spirit is a key feature of the faith of those in the circle of believers around Sutcliff, Carey, and Fuller. It is highly significant that Zechariah 4:6 ("Not by might, nor by power, but by my Spirit") was the unofficial motto of the Baptist Missionary Society after its formation in 1792.

Moreover, Sutcliff argued in his sermon, jealousy for God results in an evangelistic lifestyle. He described this lifestyle by means of Jesus' declaration in the Sermon on the Mount that the people of God are the salt of the earth and the light of the world.

> Are they [i.e., God's people] not the salt of the earth? It is not proper that the salt should lie all in one heap. It should be scattered abroad. Are they not the light of the world? These taken collectively should, like the sun, endeavor to enlighten the whole earth. As all the rays, however, that each can emit, are limited in their extent, let them be dispersed, that thus the whole globe may be illuminated. Are they not witnesses for God? It is necessary they be distributed upon every hill, and every mountain, in order that their sound may go into all the earth, and their words unto the end of the world.[4]

God's intention for the local congregation of believers is that it be an aggressive evangelistic body, seeking "to enlighten the whole earth." In commending this balance of ardent prayer and vigorous evangelistic effort, Sutcliff was not only describing what he regarded as characteristics of genuine Christianity, but he was also outlining measures he considered essential for the revival of the Calvinistic Baptist cause in

---

4   John Sutcliff, "Jealousy for the Lord of Hosts" in Haykin, *One Heart and One Soul*, 364.

England. Similarly, Carey would argue that concern for the salvation of others is a mark of true spirituality.[5]

When these marks of true jealousy for God are present, Sutcliff concluded, "this will tend to promote the interests of religion in the world. The cause of Christ will prosper; he must increase; his kingdom shall come." Yes, he reiterated, when God's people pray and evangelize, "the empire of Jesus shall advance, his kingdom arise, and the crown flourish upon his head." If this sermon was typical of Sutcliff's preaching, it is a pity that none of his other sermons have survived.

FULLER'S MISSIONARY SERMON

The second sermon preached that spring day in 1791 was that of Andrew Fuller. "The Pernicious Influence of Delay in Religious Concerns" is the intriguing title that Fuller later gave to the sermon.[6] His text was taken from the first chapter of the minor prophet Haggai: "Thus speaketh the LORD of hosts, saying, This people say, The time is not come, the time the LORD's house should be built" (Hag. 1:2). After sketching the

---

5 William Carey, *An Enquiry into the Obligations of Christians, to Use Means for the Conversion of the Heathens* (1792; repr., Didcot, Oxfordshire, England: The Baptist Missionary Society, 1991), 3.

6 When Fuller's collected works were published after his death, this title was changed to "Instances, Evil, and Tendency of Delay, in the Concerns of Religion," or something very similar. See *The Complete Works of the Rev. Andrew Fuller* (1845; repr., Harrisonburg, Va.: Sprinkle, 1988), 1:145–54. Quotations from Fuller's sermon in the pages that follow are taken from Sutcliff and Fuller, *Jealousy for the Lord of Hosts: and, The Pernicious Influence of Delay in Religious Concerns.*

historical context of this verse—namely, the refusal of the Isra-elites to get to work on rebuilding the temple after their return from the Babylonian exile—Fuller noted that the main prob-lem that afflicted the Israelites was a "procrastinating spirit." It was not, however, a problem unique to them, for it hampered both unbelievers and believers in his own day. With regard to the latter, it prevented them from "undertaking any great or good work for the cause of Christ, or the good of mankind."

Thankfully, Fuller declared in an illustration of his point, the great German Reformer Martin Luther (1483–1546) was free from this tendency. If he had not been, he and his fellow Reformers would never have undertaken "the glorious work of the Reformation" and the house of the Lord "might have lain waste to this day." Fuller was convinced that the ministry of the Reformers in word and in print had been honored by the Spirit of God for the blessing of many in the sixteenth and later centuries. The example of Luther was thus an appropri-ate one to bring forward to encourage Fuller's hearers to break out of the grip of a "procrastinating spirit."

The Reformation was undoubtedly a watershed in the history of Christianity. The rise of what has been termed the modern missionary movement at the end of the eigh-teenth century—in which Fuller, Sutcliff, Carey, and their friends played a critical role—was certainly another. From our standpoint at the beginning of the twenty-first century, it is fascinating to see these two events linked together as Fuller pressed home his point regarding the debilitating effect of procrastination on the church of his day immediately after he had mentioned the example of Luther. His hearers should seriously ponder, Fuller urged, whether it was this tendency to procrastinate that had resulted in "so few and so feeble efforts" being "made for the propagation of the gospel in the world." According to Matthew 28:19–20 and Mark 16:15, Christ gave His Apostolic band a command to evangelize the nations, something that they had sought to do with "assiduity and fidelity." But, he continued, how different was the subsequent history of the church:

> Since their days, we seem to sit down half contented that the greater part of the world should still remain in ignorance and idolatry. Some noble efforts have indeed been made; but they are small in number, when compared with the magnitude of the object. . . . We pray for the conversion and salvation of the world, and yet neglect the ordinary means by which those ends have been used to be accomplished. It pleased God, heretofore, by the foolishness of preaching, to save them that believed; and there is reason to think it will still please God to work by that distinguished means. Ought we not then at least to try by some means to convey more of the good news of salvation to the world around us than has hitherto been conveyed?[7]

---

7   Sutcliff and Fuller, *Jealousy for the Lord of Hosts: and, The Pernicious Influence of Delay in Religious Concerns*, 22–23.

By this time, Fuller had read Carey's *Enquiry into the Obligations of Christians*, which gave him a fair idea of the size of the evangelistic task that still lay before the church as well as a summary understanding of the history of missions. As this portion of his sermon indicates, he had obviously been deeply challenged by his reading of it, and his awareness of Matthew 28:19–20 as an evangelistic text was firmly established.

Furthermore, since 1784, the entire Northamptonshire Baptist Association had been regularly praying for revival and the worldwide advance of the gospel.[8] Were Fuller and his hearers in earnest when they prayed this request? If so, how could they continue to pray along these lines without giving serious thought to its fulfillment? If its fulfillment were to come, Fuller now contended, it would be through God's time-honored method of planting churches and winning the lost: preaching. Fuller was cognizant that Scripture gives preaching primacy of place in evangelism. Immediately after the concluding question in the quote above, Fuller cited Romans 10:13–15, in which the Apostle Paul shows that it is impossible for either Jew or Gentile to embrace Christ as Savior without hearing the proclamation of the gospel. Particularly germane to Fuller's argument was verse 15, where Paul asks how such preaching shall take place unless preachers be sent.

---

8   See Haykin, *One Heart and One Soul*, 153–71.

Response to the Clipston Sermons

After hearing these two sermons, those gathered in the Clipston meetinghouse were sobered and deeply convicted. Nearly twenty-five years later, John Webster Morris could still recall the way in which the meetinghouse was pervaded with a "deep solemnity" and how the entire congregation was overwhelmed by what it had heard.[9] Carey must have been thrilled by what he had just heard and was determined to strike while the iron was hot. After dinner at midday, he forcefully urged those present to make some decision concerning "a society for propagating the gospel among the heathen." A discussion then ensued that lasted most of the afternoon.

In the discussion, Carey obviously would have emphasized that the logical implication of what Sutcliff and Fuller had said during the day was what he had urged in the conclusion of his yet-unpublished *Enquiry into the Obligations of Christians*: they should form a missionary society for taking the gospel to lands overseas. Carey's friends and fellow ministers were not averse to what he was pressing upon them, but they felt that forming such a society was, in Fuller's words, "something too great, and too much like grasping at an object utterly beyond their reach."[10]

---

9 Morris, *Memoirs of the Life and Writings of the Rev. Andrew Fuller* (1816), 98.

10 Eustace Carey, *Memoir of William Carey, D.D.* (London: Jackson and Walford, 1836), 73–74.

Caution from Sutcliff
and Benjamin Beddome

Sutcliff in particular, we are told, cautioned against haste.[11] Is it not ironic that Sutcliff, who only that morning had called for aggressive evangelism, urged caution at the end of the day when Carey's plan to implement such evangelism was placed on the table? What undoubtedly caused Sutcliff to be so cautious was not the issue of evangelism per se—he himself had been involved in village preaching for more than a decade— but the question of support from their sister churches. Would the Baptist churches in their association and throughout the nation, few of them wealthy, influential establishments, be able and willing to implement Carey's vision?

Carey and his friends could expect, of course, some degree of opposition from those still solidly entrenched in hyper-Calvinism. But it was not the disapproval from these quarters that made Sutcliff hesitate to implement Carey's vision. It was the concerns that would be expressed by those who shared his and Carey's evangelical Calvinism. Such concerns were typified by the respected Baptist Benjamin Beddome (1718–95), pastor of the Particular Baptist cause in Bourton-on-the-Water, Gloucestershire.[12]

---

11 Morris, *Memoirs of the Life and Writings of the Rev. Andrew Fuller*, 99.

12 The earliest biographical account of Beddome's life is an extensive obituary written by John Rippon: "Rev. Benjamin Beddome, A.M. Bourton-on-the-Water, Gloucesteshire," *Baptist Annual Register* 2 (1794–97): 314–26. An especially significant biographical study can be found in Thomas Brooks, *Pictures of the Past: The History of the Baptist Church, Bourton-on-the-Water* (London: Judd & Glass, 1861), 21–66.

Writing to Fuller in 1793, Beddome told him that his "scheme," that is, the formation of a missionary society, was definitely ill advised. "Considering the paucity of well-qualified ministers," he reckoned that it had a "very unfavourable aspect with respect to destitute churches" in Britain, where, after all, he said, "charity ought to begin." As for Carey, he told Fuller:

I had the pleasure once to see and hear Mr. Carey. It struck me that he was the most suitable person in the kingdom, at least whom I knew, to supply my place and make up my great deficiencies when either disabled or removed. A different plan is formed and pursued, and I fear that the great and good man, though influenced by the most excellent motives, will meet with a disappointment. However, God hath his ends and whoever is disappointed he will not [be], he cannot be so. My unbelieving heart is ready to suggest with the Jews of old that "the time is not come that the Lord's house should be built" [Haggai 1:2].

Beddome had serious reservations about Carey's going to India, but he was prepared to admit that he might be wrong, that God's plans might be quite different from what he envisioned. He also confessed that the prophet Haggai's censure of

---

See also Michael A.G. Haykin, "Benjamin Beddome (1717–1795): His Life and His Hymns" in John H.Y. Briggs, ed., *Pulpit and People: Studies in Eighteenth Century Baptist Life and Thought* (Milton Keynes, England: Paternoster, 2009), 93–111.

the Jews of his day for unbelief might well be applied to him. It is fascinating that this confession contained an allusion to the very passage on which Fuller had preached a couple of years earlier at Clipston, when he called upon his fellow Baptists to exercise a deeper trust in God. Had Beddome read Fuller's sermon, and was he indicating how it applied to him?[13]

William Carey's great-grandson, his biographer S. Pearce Carey, has expressed the opinion that of "all the Association's young leaders none exercised a weightier influence" than Sutcliff.[14] Definitely, that afternoon in Clipston his advice to wait was followed. The only decision that was made was to recommend that Carey revise the *Enquiry into the Obligations of Christians* with a view to publication, which would, it was hoped, help to sound out the attitude of the "religious public" regarding a missionary endeavor.[15]

A number of the ministers stayed in the Clipston manse that night. Carey, Fuller, Morris, and possibly Sutcliff sat up chatting till well after midnight. The implementation of Carey's vision and the way that God had spoken through the preaching gave them much to talk about. Despite the fact that they had already had supper, around one o'clock Fuller felt

---

13 It is noteworthy that John Newton, who came to have a deep admiration for Carey, had his doubts initially about the mission. As he wrote to Ryland on May 2, 1794: "Your India Mission has my prayers and best wishes. I hope some good may be done by detached and occasional attempts, but I think the Lord's time, for great things is not yet fully come." Cited in Grant Gordon, "The Impact of John Newton on William Carey and the BMS" (Unpublished paper, [1992]), 7.

14 S. Pearce Carey, *William Carey*, 8th ed. (London: Carey, 1934), 68.

15 Carey, *Memoir of William Carey*, 74.

hungry and asked Morris if he had any more meat. When Morris told him that he did, Fuller told him to get it, and they would roast it in the fire that was still blazing on the hearth. As the meat sizzled and cooked, the Baptist pastors continued to chat and listen to Carey elaborate on his vision of a missionary society. The decision of the afternoon was not modified by this late-night discussion and nocturnal repast, but what took place in the manse that night was long remembered as a fitting conclusion to an eventful day.[16]

AN ENQUIRY INTO THE OBLIGATIONS OF CHRISTIANS

William Carey wrote one truly seminal work, *An Enquiry into the Obligations of Christians, to Use Means for the Conversion of the Heathens* (1792). With a minimum of emotional coloring and rhetoric, this tract argued that the mandate that Christ laid upon the church in Matthew 28:18–20 to evangelize the nations is binding for all time. It was thus incumbent upon local churches of Carey's day to determine what were the appropriate means for accomplishing the task. While it does not appear to have been a best seller at the time of its publication, this tract aptly argued that "the missionary obligation of the church is of permanent validity and grounded in the sovereign redemptive purpose of God."[17]

---

16 Pearce Carey, *William Carey*, 70.

17 B. Stanley, "Carey, William" in Timothy Larsen et al., eds., *Biographical Dictionary of Evangelicals* (Leicester, England: Inter-Varsity Press, 2003), 119.

When this tract was published in 1792, it contained five sections. In the first, Carey tackled head-on the theological objections raised by hyper-Calvinists to the evangelization of other nations. Some argued that the mandate to evangelize the nations as found in Matthew 28 was required only of the Apostles and that they had actually fulfilled it in their lifetime. In fact, this line of argument was not uncommon in various European Protestant circles, where it was supported by reference to proof texts such as Romans 10:18, Mark 16:20, and Colossians 1:23.[18] A more pragmatic line of reasoning also declared that there was "enough to do to attend to the salvation of our own countrymen" without sailing to the ends of the earth.[19]

Carey's response to the first of these arguments was drawn directly from Matthew 28:18–20. If the commission with regard to evangelism applied only to the Apostles, should not this also be the case for the direction to baptize those who became Christ's disciples? Since Carey's tract had as its principal audience fellow Baptists who obviously took very seriously the command to baptize, this would have been

---

18 John Appleby has argued that John Owen maintained a similar view in *The True Nature of a Gospel Church and Its Government* in *The Works of John Owen*, ed. William H. Goold (1850–53; repr., Edinburgh, Scotland: Banner of Truth, 1968), 16:92–93, where Owen appears to insist that local churches do not have the power to ordain a man to conduct evangelism in an area where there are no churches. See John Appleby, *"I Can Plod . . .": William Carey and the Early Years of the First Baptist Missionary Society* (London: Grace Publications Trust, 2007), 63–64. B.S. Poh, on the other hand, believes that Appleby has misread Owen at this point. See his "2016/3: A Review of 'I Can Plod,'" *Gospel Highway*, https://www.ghmag.net/articles/2016-articles/20163-i-can-plod.

19 Carey, *Enquiry into the Obligations of Christians*, 35–36.

a telling point. Then, what of those individuals who have gone to other nations and planted local churches? If the hyper-Calvinists were correct, they must have gone without God's authorization. Yet, as Carey demonstrated in section 2 of the tract, God had been with these men and women and had blessed their efforts. Finally, Christ's promise to be with His church till the end of time made little sense if the command to evangelize the world was to be completed by the end of the first century.[20]

Turning to the argument that there was enough to do at home, Carey readily agreed that there were "thousands in our own land as far from God as possible." This state of affairs ought to spur the Baptists on to yet greater efforts to plant local churches throughout Britain, from which the gospel could be faithfully proclaimed and these thousands reached. Yet, it still remained a fact that most of the nations of the world of that day had no copies of the Scriptures in their own tongues and no means of hearing the faithful proclamation of the Word.[21] In this section of the tract, Carey showed that missionary work was not reserved for a bygone era but was the present duty of the church. As one of the key words of the tract's title stated, Christians had an obligation to engage in mission.

---

20 Carey, *Enquiry into the Obligations of Christians*, 8–9.
21 Carey, *Enquiry into the Obligations of Christians*, 13.

A Mini-History of Missions

Section 2 of the tract traced the history of missions down to Carey's own day, which demonstrated that God had blessed missionary endeavors beyond the Apostolic era. Carey cited texts from such patristic authors as Justin Martyr (c. 100–155), Irenaeus (c. 130–c. 202), and Tertullian (c. 170–c. 215), as well as making reference to various figures in late antiquity such as Patrick (c. 389–c. 460), who, according to Carey's reckoning, was "useful, and laid the foundations of several churches in Ireland."[22] Medieval Christendom, though, came to be marked by "blind zeal, gross superstition, and infamous cruelties," such that "the professors of Christ needed conversion, as much as the heathen world."[23] Carey regarded the preaching and writings of John Wycliffe (c. 1330–84), which were "the means of the conversion of great numbers," as the beginning of the recovery of the gospel that continued in the sixteenth century as the Reformation.[24]

In the seventeenth and early eighteenth centuries, Carey singled out John Eliot (1604–90) in New England and Bartholomäus Ziegenbalg (1682–1719) in South India as having been "useful" in missionary endeavors. And given his love for Edwards, it is not surprising that he mentioned David Brainerd (1718–47), whose life and labors were immortalized by

22 Carey, *Enquiry into the Obligations of Christians*, 29–30 and 32.

23 Carey, *Enquiry into the Obligations of Christians*, 34.

24 Carey, *Enquiry into the Obligations of Christians*, 35.

Edwards' biographical study of him, as having had "wonderful success" in his ministry.[25] The impact that Brainerd's life made upon Carey can also be gauged by his closing remarks to this missionary tract:

> It is true all the reward is of mere grace, but it is never-theless encouraging; what a treasure, what an harvest must await such characters as Paul, and Elliot [sic], and Brainerd, and others, who have given themselves wholly to the work of the Lord. What a heaven will it be to see the many myriads of poor heathens, of Brit-ons amongst the rest, who by their labours have been brought to the knowledge of God. Surely a crown of rejoicing like this is worth aspiring to. Surely it is worth while to lay ourselves out with all our might, in promoting the cause, and kingdom of Christ.[26]

THE UNEQUALED EXAMPLE
OF THE MORAVIANS

Of particular note in this mini-history of missions are Carey's remarks about the Moravians and their evangelistic efforts: "None of the moderns have equalled the Moravian Breth-ren in this good work; they have sent missions to Greenland,

---

25 Carey, *Enquiry into the Obligations of Christians*, 36–37. For the impact of Eliot and Brainerd on Carey and his ministry, see Timothy George, *Faithful Witness: The Life and Mission of William Carey* (Birmingham, Ala.: New Hope, 1991), 42–45.

26 Carey, *Enquiry into the Obligations of Christians*, 87.

Labrador, and several of the West Indian islands, which have been blessed for good."[27] The Moravians were the spiritual descendants of the Czech reformer Jan Hus (c.1372–1415). After a powerful movement of the Holy Spirit in the midst of their community at Herrnhut in Saxony, Germany, in August 1727, they became the most active Protestant missionary community of the eighteenth century and played a key role in the evangelical revivals in the transatlantic world.[28]

From Herrnhut, eighteenth-century Moravian missionaries went out literally to the four corners of the earth: to the West Indies in 1732; to Greenland in 1733; to Lapland and the colony of Georgia in 1734; to Surinam in 1735; to South Africa in 1737; to Algeria in 1739; to the Native Americans, Sri Lanka, and Romania in 1740; and to Persia in 1747. By 1760, no fewer than 226 missionaries had been sent out by this tiny community. Looking back on this amazing outburst of missionary energy, William Wilberforce could say of the Moravians at the end of the eighteenth century: "They are

---

27 Carey, *Enquiry into the Obligations of Christians*, 37.

28 For a succinct account of the Moravians, see especially John R. Weinlick and Albert H. Frank, *The Moravian Church through the Ages*, rev. ed. (Bethlehem, Pa.: The Moravian Church in America, 1996). For the impact of the Moravians on the modern missionary movement, see Kenneth B. Mulholland, "From Luther to Carey: Pietism and the Modern Missionary Movement," *Bibliotheca Sacra* 156, no. 621 (January–March 1999): 85–95, and Kenneth B. Mulholland, "Moravians, Puritans, and the Modern Missionary Movement," *Bibliotheca Sacra* 156, no. 622 (April–June 1999): 221–32. David A. Schattschnieder has explored the influence of the Moravians on Carey: "William Carey, Modern Missions, and the Moravian Influence," *International Bulletin of Missionary Research* 22, no. 1 (January 1998): 8–11. He notes, though, "I have not yet been able to verify that Carey ever actually met a Moravian" (9).

a body who have perhaps excelled all mankind in solid and unequivocal proofs of the love of Christ and of ardent, active zeal in his service. It is a zeal tempered with prudence, softened with meekness and supported by a courage which no danger can intimidate and a quiet certainty no hardship can exhaust."[29] Given this remarkable missionary movement, it is no wonder that Carey wrote to Sutcliff in January 1798:

> I rejoice much at the missionary spirit which has lately gone forth: surely it is a prelude to a universal spread of the Gospel! Your account of the German Moravian Brethren's affectionate regards towards me is very pleasing. I am not much moved by what men in general say of me; yet I cannot be insensible to the regards of men eminent for godliness.[30]

As to the overall significance of this mini-history, missiologist Andrew Walls rightly observes, "Carey saw himself and those whom he was stirring to action as entering into a process already in motion, not as initiating that process."[31]

---

29 Cited in Colin A. Grant, "Europe's Moravians—A Pioneer Missionary Church," *Evangelical Missions Quarterly* 12 (1976): 221.

30 William Carey, Letter to John Sutcliff, January 16, 1798, Baptist Missionary Society Archives, Angus Library, Regent's Park College, University of Oxford, England; box IN 13.

31 Andrew F. Walls, "The Protestant Missionary Awakening in Its European Context" in his ed., *The Cross-Cultural Process in Christian History: Studies in the Transmission and Appropriation of Faith* (Maryknoll, N.Y.: Orbis, 2002), 204.

Sections 3 and 4

Following this mini-history of missions was a section primarily composed of a statistical table of all the countries of the then-known world, detailing their length and breadth in miles, the size of their respective populations, and the religious affiliation of the majority of their inhabitants. None of this was guesswork. It was the fruit of many hours spent scouring the latest geographical handbooks and the *Northampton Mercury*, the local newspaper, for facts and notices about the nations of the world.[32] From this spare table of facts and figures, Carey concluded that the vast majority of the world was sunk in "the most deplorable state of heathen darkness, without any means of knowing the true God, except what are afforded them by the works of nature" and "utterly destitute of the knowledge of the gospel of Christ."[33] From one angle, this section is a list of statistics. But Carey's words just cited show, as Timothy George has rightly noted, that for Carey, the men and women of these foreign lands were "not mere statistics"; on the contrary, "they were *persons*, eternal souls destined to live forever in the bliss of heaven or the darkness of hell."[34]

The fourth section of the tract demolished the practical obstacles that Carey's contemporaries were wont to raise

---

32 Ernest A. Payne, "Introduction" to William Carey, *An Enquiry into the Obligations of Christians, to Use Means for the Conversion of the Heathens* (1792; repr. Didcot, England: The Baptist Missionary Society, 1991), 20–21.

33 Carey, *Enquiry into the Obligations of Christians*, 62–63.

34 George, *Faithful Witness*, 22.

in response to what he was proposing. Confronting the real problems posed by keeping life going in other nations of the world—their distance from Britain, their different languages, their supposed "barbarism," and their purported treatment of Europeans—Carey cogently argued that none of these rendered the evangelization of these nations impossible.[35]

Praying for the Advance of the Gospel

The final section of the tract, section 5, concentrates on outlining what was entailed in another key word from the work's title: *means*. First in importance among these means is "fervent and united prayer."

> One of the first, and most important of those duties which are incumbent upon us, is fervent and united prayer. However the influence of the Holy Spirit may be set at nought, and run down by many, it will be found upon trial, that all means which we can use, without it, will be ineffectual. If a temple is raised for God in the heathen world, it will not be "by might, nor by power," nor by the authority of the magistrate, or the eloquence of the orator; but "by my Spirit, saith the Lord of Hosts"

---

35 Carey, *Enquiry into the Obligations of Christians*, 67–76.

[Zech. 4:6]. We must therefore be in real earnest in supplicating his blessing upon our labors.[36]

As Andrew Walls has noted, this text cannot be fully appreciated apart from the background of prayer meetings for revival that had been going on since 1784 in the Baptist circles in which Carey was moving. Carey was thoroughly convinced from the record of Scripture and the history of the church that "the most glorious works of grace that ever took place, have been in answer to prayer."[37] Prayer therefore had to be the first resource or means that the church used to fulfill Christ's mandate. Further proof of Carey's conviction in this regard was the fact that he and Fuller, Sutcliff, and Ryland made it a point during these years to meet once a month for an entire day of fasting and prayer for revival.[38]

This paragraph is also a determined repudiation of reliance upon two sources of power that have commonly been used in the history of Christian missions: political power and rational argumentation. As Brian Stanley has pointed out, both of these were strong temptations for nineteenth-century British missions strategists: "the leaky umbrella of imperial power . . . and the Enlightenment expectation that Christian

---

36 Carey, *Enquiry into the Obligations of Christians*, 77.

37 Andrew F. Walls, "Missionary Societies and the Fortunate Subversion of the Church," *The Evangelical Quarterly* 60 (1988): 144; Carey, *Enquiry into the Obligations of Christians*, 78–79.

38 Joshua Marshman, *The Efficiency of Divine Grace: A Funeral Sermon for the Late Rev. William Carey, D.D.* (Serampore, India: Serampore, 1834), 24.

rational apologetic would convince people of the superiority of Christianity."[39] Carey belonged to a tradition of Christian spirituality that emphasized the power of the Spirit and that stretched back through mid-eighteenth-century evangelicals such as George Whitefield and Jonathan Edwards to Puritans such as John Owen.

THE NECESSITY OF ACTION

Prayer was vital, but, Carey argued, there were other means that Christians could employ. Turning to the world of eighteenth-century commerce for an analogy, Carey noted the way in which merchants would form trading companies, outfit ships with care, and then, venturing all, "cross the widest and most tempestuous seas," face inhospitable climates, fears, and other hardships to successfully secure material wealth. They do such things "because their souls enter into the spirit of the project, and their happiness in a manner depends on its success."[40] The truest interest of Christians, on the other hand, lies in the extension of their Lord's kingdom. Carey thus made the following suggestion:

> Suppose a company of serious Christians, ministers and private persons, were to form themselves into a society, and make a number of rules respecting the regulation

---

39 Stanley, "Carey, William," 119.
40 Carey, *Enquiry into the Obligations of Christians*, 81–82.

of the plan, and the persons who are to be employed as missionaries, the means of defraying the expense, etc., etc. This society must consist of persons whose hearts are in the work, men of serious religion, and possessing a spirit of perseverance; there must be a determination not to admit any person who is not of this description, or to retain him longer than he answers to it.[41]

Out of the members of this society a small committee could be established that would oversee such things as gathering information, collecting funds, selecting missionaries, and equipping them for missions overseas.[42] "All of this sounds so trite today," Walls comments, "because we are used to the paraphernalia of committees and councils of reference and subscriptions and donations." To Baptist churches in the eighteenth century, however, all of this would have been quite new and, in some ways, quite extraordinary. Carey had no desire to subvert the primacy of the local church, but he had grasped the simple fact that the way that Baptist congregations were then organized made it next to impossible for them to engage effectively in missions overseas.[43] Here, Carey was drawing upon a tradition in English Protestant circles in which voluntary religious associations were formed in order to achieve specific goals.

---

41 Carey, *Enquiry into the Obligations of Christians*, 82–83.
42 Carey, *Enquiry into the Obligations of Christians*, 83–86.
43 Walls, "Missionary Societies," 146.

What is central to Carey's vision here is his conviction that the success of a missionary endeavor is deeply tied to the oneness of heart and purpose of those who undertake it. In fact, is this not true of all historical advances for the kingdom of God? If those involved, for instance, in church planting or missional activities or theological education do not share a oneness of heart and vision and have an insuperable love for one another, will not the endeavor fail? But God had yoked Carey to friends—Sutcliff, Fuller, and Ryland—who would not fail him.

CHAPTER FOUR

Going to India and the Need for Friends

The formation of a missionary society, for which Carey had cogently argued at the conclusion of his *Enquiry into the Obligations of Christians*, had been delayed, but it could not be put off indefinitely. When the association met in 1792, the year after the tract's publication, at Friar Lane Baptist Church, Nottingham, Carey's *Enquiry* gave added force to his pleadings that the association brook no further delay. The association had never met this far north before, and for some of the messengers to the assembly it meant a horse ride of sixty or seventy miles. Due to this distance, some of the churches, including Olney, sent only their pastor to represent them. The church building in which they met was Nottingham's sole Calvinistic Baptist meetinghouse.[1] It was a plain white building, well-lit

---

1   S. Pearce Carey, *William Carey*, 8th ed. (London: Carey, 1934), 80–81; Sidney F. Clark, "Nottingham Baptist Beginnings," *The Baptist Quarterly* 17 (1957–58): 165.

and spacious, able to seat around 230 people. Unlike some of the settings for earlier association meetings, the meetinghouse this year was able to accommodate comfortably the congregation that assembled for the public services. Due to the location, the number of those attending was definitely down from previous years. This building would be sold in 1815, and in the course of the nineteenth century it came to be used as a secondhand furniture store. It has since been demolished.

The "Deathless Sermon"

The first public meeting of the assembly was at ten o'clock a.m. on Wednesday, May 30. Sutcliff outlined the day's agenda and led in prayer, and then Carey came to the pulpit to preach. The text on which he had chosen to speak was Isaiah 54:2–3, which reads thus in the King James Version: "Enlarge the place of thy tent, and let them stretch forth the curtains of thine habitations: spare not, lengthen thy cords, and strengthen thy stakes; for thou shalt break forth on the right hand and on the left; and thy seed shall inherit the Gentiles, and make the desolate cities to be inhabited." Exactly how Carey came to choose this text is not known. Iain H. Murray has recently echoed the plausible suggestion that William Cowper's hymn "Jesus Where'er Thy People Meet," which was composed in late March or early April 1769, had drawn Carey's attention to the Isaiah text. Believers in the Midlands had been singing this hymn since 1779. Its fifth stanza runs:

Behold! at thy commanding word,
We stretch the curtain and the cord;
Come thou, and fill this wider space,
And bless us with a large increase.[2]

Although we do not know for certain what led Carey to this passage, the verses from Isaiah had a message for his day and his circle of friends. They needed to trust God and venture forth to the nations with the message of the gospel, confident that God would bless that message and extend His kingdom. Nor do we know the details of the sermon that Carey preached, since no copy of the sermon exists. What we do know are the two main divisions of his message that morning: "Let us expect great things" and "Let us attempt great things." This is the way that Andrew Fuller referred to the substance of Carey's sermon in what is the earliest written reference to it, a letter to the York-shire Baptist John Fawcett dated August 30, 1793.[3] These two divisions would later be embellished as "Expect great things from God" and "Attempt great things for God." However, as A. Christopher Smith has shown, his original challenge was simply "expect great things; attempt great things."[4] His close friends—Sutcliff, Fuller, and Ryland—were quite prepared to

---

2 *The Poems of William Cowper*, eds. John D. Baird and Charles Ryskamp (Oxford, England: Clarendon, 1980), I:166; Iain H. Murray, "William Carey: Climbing the Rainbow," *The Banner of Truth* 349 (October 1992): 17.

3 Cited by A. Christopher Smith, "The Spirit and Letter of Carey's Catalytic Watchword. A Study in the Transmission of Baptist Tradition," *The Baptist Quarterly* 33 (1989–90): 227.

4 Smith, "The Spirit and Letter of Carey's Catalytic Watchword," 226–37.

"expect great things" from God's hand. As the sermons that Sutcliff and Fuller gave in April 1791 at Clipston reveal, they were also ready to talk about attempting "great things" for the glory of God. But Carey knew that Scripture (e.g., James 1:22) would have them move beyond words to action. They had to actually "attempt great things."

The effect of Carey's sermon was shattering and considerable. A year or so later, Fuller wrote to John Fawcett about the ongoing impact of what came to be called the "Deathless Sermon" of Carey: "I feel the use of his sermon to this day. Let us pray much, hope much, expect much, labor much; an eternal weight of glory awaits us."[5] At the time, Carey's sermon had convinced his friends of "the criminality of [their] supineness in the cause of God." If the entire congregation had broken into profuse weeping, Ryland later said, he would not have been surprised.[6] The meeting the following morning was held at six, not long after sunrise. There was a time of sharing Christian experience, in which, as Fuller put it, "they yearned to feel each other's spirits."[7]

Afterward there was the business meeting of the assembly. It was decided to give five guineas to those seeking to secure "the abolition of the inhuman and ungodly trade in the persons of men." It bears noting that along with some three

---

5 Andrew Fuller, letter to John Fawcett, August 30, 1793, cited in Timothy George, *Faithful Witness: The Life and Mission of William Carey* (Birmingham, Ala.: New Hope, 1991), 33.

6 Ryland, *The Life and Death of the Rev. Andrew Fuller*, 150.

7 Pearce Carey, *William Carey*, 85.

hundred thousand people in Great Britain, Carey gave up sugar around this time since it was obtained from slave labor in the West Indies. Thus, in his words, he cleansed his "hands of blood."[8] Moreover, during the entire time that he was in India, from 1793 till his death over forty years later, he regularly pleaded with God in prayer for the destruction of slavery. In no public question did he take a deeper interest. And when the slaves were finally freed in 1833, his eyes apparently filled with tears as he gave thanks to God, and he proposed that for an entire month the Serampore Mission should give special thanksgiving to God in all of their meetings.[9]

Then some money was given to help defray the expenses of four of the messengers to the association who came from "distant and poorer churches." Finally, monies were provided to support the preaching of the gospel in Derby and Braybrooke, a village eight or so miles northwest of Kettering. Imagine Carey's surprise when, despite the impact that his sermon had wrought the day before, the assembly was going to dismiss without any decisive action being taken with regard to missions overseas. According to John Clark Marshman, the son of Joshua Marshman, Carey's valued colleague at Serampore, a deeply distressed Carey turned to Fuller, seized him by

---

8   William Carey, *An Enquiry into the Obligations of Christians, to Use Means for the Conversion of the Heathens* (1792; repr., London: Baptist Missionary Society, 1934), 86. For a mention of this boycott of slave-grown sugar, see Charles Colson with Ellen Santilli Vaughn, *Kingdoms in Conflict* (New York: William Morrow & Co., 1987), 103.

9   Ernest A. Payne, *Freedom in Jamaica: Some Chapters in the Story of the Baptist Missionary Society*, rev. ed. (London: Carey, 1946), 43.

the hand, and asked whether they were going to disperse once again without doing anything. Whatever further reservations Fuller, or, for that matter, Sutcliff and Ryland, may have had, they were once for all swept away in this "catalytic moment in the history of the church." These three men knew in their hearts that they could not put Carey off any longer. Before they left that day, they and the other messengers to the association had resolved to draw up plans at the ministerial meeting that October for forming a "Baptist society for propagating the gospel among the heathens."[10]

Forming the Baptist Missionary Society

This ministerial meeting was held in Kettering on October 2. The previous evening and all that day, the weather had been signaling the approach of winter. William Cowper, now living about twenty miles away in Weston Underwood, wrote that day of the "sky all in sables."[11] The inclement weather, though, did nothing to dampen the ardor of those ministers who gathered that day in Kettering.

Fuller's mind, for one, was certainly not on the weather.

---

10 John Clark Marshman, *The Life and Times of Carey, Marshman, and Ward* (1859; repr. Serampore, India: Council of Serampore College, 2005), 1:15; George, *Faithful Witness*, 33; "Breviates" in John Ryland, *Godly Zeal, Described and Recommended* (Nottingham, England, 1792), 16.

11 William Cowper, Letter to William Hayley, October 2, 1792, in *The Letters and Prose Writings of William Cowper*, eds. James King and Charles Ryskamp (Oxford, England: Clarendon, 1984), IV:205.

The months since the association meetings in Nottingham had been very trying ones for him personally. A few days after he got back from Nottingham, his wife, Sarah (1756–92), began to experience bouts of insanity, till by July she was "as destitute of reason as an infant." She became convinced that Fuller was not her husband, that he was an "imposter, who had entered the house, and taken possession of every place, and of all that belonged to her and her husband." Moreover, she was convinced that she was no longer at home, but was in the house of strangers. The doors of the house had to be kept locked, since she tried to escape a number of times. She was thus reduced to walking up and down through the house, bemoaning her lot, and crying out that she was lost and ruined. All this time she was expecting. About two weeks before she delivered the child, a daughter whom Fuller called Bathoni, she recovered her senses for a little over twelve hours. Then, suddenly, while they were eating dinner at midday, her mind was gone again, and in that state she remained till her death a few hours later on August 23. Their daughter lived less than a month.[12]

Though beset with grief over the deaths of his wife and child, Fuller found himself having to provide leadership for what was an unprecedented step among Calvinistic Baptists—the formation of a missionary society. After the public services of October 2 were concluded, Fuller and thirteen

---

12 Andrew Fuller, Letter to John Ryland, July 9, 1792, in Ryland, *Life and Death of the Rev. Andrew Fuller*, 286; Andrew Fuller, Letter to Stephen Gardiner, August 25, 1792, in Ryland, *Life and Death of the Rev. Andrew Fuller*, 286–91.

other men—eleven pastors, a deacon from Fuller's congregation, and a ministerial student—crowded into the back parlor
of the home of a Martha Wallis, a longstanding member of
the Kettering church. Her back parlor measured twelve feet by
ten, ample space for three or four men to sit and stretch out
their legs, but quite a tight squeeze for fourteen. Her home,
though, was no stranger to numerous guests. Over the years,
so many preachers had stayed there that Carey appropriately
dubbed the house the "Gospel Inn."

In addition to Fuller, Ryland, Sutcliff, and Carey, there
was also there that night Samuel Pearce (1766–99), whose
church in Birmingham belonged to the Midland Association,
but whom Fuller had invited to be one of the preachers that
day. Although Pearce is scarcely remembered now, in his own
day, both within and without Baptist circles, he was deeply
respected for the power of his preaching and the depth of his
spirituality. William Jay (1769–1853), the Congregationalist
minister of Bath and no mean judge of character, once wrote
of Pearce's preaching, "When I have endeavored to form an
image of our Lord as a preacher, Pearce has oftener presented
himself to my mind than any other I have been acquainted
with." And referring to the last time that he saw Pearce alive,
Jay had this comment: "What a savour does communion
with such a man leave upon the spirit."[13] His preaching and

---

13 *The Autobiography of William Jay*, eds. George Redford and John Angell James
(1854; repr. Edinburgh: Banner of Truth, 1974), 372, 373. On Pearce, see also
Michael A.G. Haykin, *Joy Unspeakable and Full of Glory: The Piety of Samuel and
Sarah Pearce* (Kitchener, Ontario: Joshua, 2012). Fuller's most popular work was his

spirituality were vital to the establishment of the Baptist Missionary Society.

Pearce had not been able to make it to Nottingham the previous May. No doubt either Fuller or Carey had filled Pearce in on the details of what had transpired at the Nottingham meetings. Of the seven other pastors who were wedged into the Wallis back parlor that night, they were, as S. Pearce Carey bluntly put it, men "of no fame and of scantiest salary," who were really "nobodies from nowhere."[14] Yet, there is one other thing that bears noting: apart from one man, Edward Sharman, they were also faithful to their calling to the ends of their lives and labored for God's approval, not that of men. Sharman was Carey's successor at Moulton, but eventually he turned against those with whom he had founded the Baptist Missionary Society. By 1800 he had become a Unitarian and had published a number of tracts against Fuller's Trinitarianism.

The ministerial student present at this historic event was William Staughton (1770–1829), who was studying at Bristol Baptist Academy. He was preaching in Northampton for a number of Sundays during September and October, and thus he was able to attend the ministerial meeting at Kettering on October 2. A year later, a love affair caused him to leave England for the United States, where he eventually had two

memoir of Pearce. See Michael A.G. Haykin, ed., *Memoirs of the Rev. Samuel Pearce*, The Complete Works of Andrew Fuller, vol. 4 (Berlin: Walter de Gruyter, 2017).

14 S. Pearce Carey, *Samuel Pearce, M.A., The Baptist Brainerd* (London: Carey, [1913]), 134; S. Pearce Carey, *William Carey*, 91.

outstanding pastorates in the city of Philadelphia and later served as the first president of Columbian College (known since 1904 as George Washington University) from 1822 to 1827. A tireless advocate of missions, he stayed in touch with Carey throughout his life, which Carey deeply appreciated. Writing in November 1817, Carey told him: "I have omitted writing to you till I am ashamed: yet it has not arisen from indifference to you, but from absolute inability for want of time. . . . You are dear to me, and have been ever since we first met together, a little before my first sailing to this country."[15]

Crammed into Martha Wallis' parlor, these fourteen men resolved to form what they called "The Particular Baptist Society for Propagating the Gospel amongst the Heathen" (it would be renamed the Baptist Missionary Society before the close of the century). In order to help finance the new venture, they each pledged to give a small sum, Fuller collecting the pledges in his snuff box. With a representation of the Apostle Paul's conversion finely embossed upon its lid, the snuff box must have seemed a fitting repository for the pledges. None of the men present that night was wealthy, but they promised to give sacrificially. Even then the pledges amounted only to thirteen pounds, two shillings, and six pence, a paltry sum on which to launch a missionary enterprise. It was truly a case of God's choosing "what is weak in the world to shame

---

15 William Carey, letter to William Staughton, November 25, 1817, cited by Roger Hayden, "Kettering 1792 and Philadelphia 1814," *The Baptist Quarterly* 21, no. 2 (April 1965): 64–65.

the strong" (1 Cor. 1:27). An executive committee including Ryland, Carey, and Sutcliff, with Fuller as secretary, was also appointed.

Fuller would remain as secretary till his death in 1815. The work of the mission consumed an enormous amount of Fuller's time as he regularly toured the country, representing the mission and raising funds. On average, he was away from home three months out of the year. Between 1798 and 1813, for instance, he made five lengthy trips to Scotland for the mission as well as undertaking journeys to Wales and Ireland.[16] He also carried on an extensive correspondence both with the missionaries in the field and with supporters at home. Finally, he supervised the selection of missionary appointees and sought to deal with troubles as they emerged on the field.[17] The amount of energy and time this took deeply worried his friends. As Robert Hall Jr. (1764–1831) put it in a letter to John Ryland Jr.: "If he [Fuller] is not more careful he will be in danger of wearing himself out before his time. His journeys, his studies, his correspondcies [sic] must be too much for the constitution of any man."[18] In fact, so heartily did he

---

16 On Fuller's trips to Scotland, see Dudley Reeves, "Andrew Fuller in Scotland," *The Banner of Truth* 106–7 (July/August 1972): 33–40; Michael A.G. Haykin, "Andrew Fuller and His Scottish Friends," *History Scotland* 15, no. 6 (November/December 2015): 24–30.

17 Doyle L. Young, "Andrew Fuller and the Modern Mission Movement," *Baptist History and Heritage* 17 (1982): 17–27.

18 Robert Hall to John Ryland Jr., May 25, 1801, cited in Geoffrey F. Nuttall, "Letters from Robert Hall to John Ryland 1791–1824," *The Baptist Quarterly* 34 (1991–92): 127.

give himself to the work of the society that after his death J. Webster Morris judged that "he lived and died a martyr to the mission."[19]

John Thomas

Carey became the society's first appointee, along with John Thomas (1757–1801), a doctor who had trained at Westminster Hospital, London.[20] In the 1780s, Thomas had run into financial difficulties and decided to escape his debts by taking the position of surgeon on one of the ships of the East India Company. During his second voyage to India in 1786, Thomas became friends with Charles Grant (1746–1823), an Anglican evangelical who was on the board of trade of the East India Company and who was based in Calcutta. Deeply moved by the wretchedness, both spiritual and material, of many of the Indian people that he saw in Calcutta, Thomas longed to alleviate their plight. Grant helped Thomas with finances to start a missionary enterprise in Bengal, where Thomas began to learn Bengali, began to translate the Scriptures into that tongue, and also make some headway in learning Sanskrit.

But by 1790, a serious rift had developed between Thomas and Grant due to the former's ongoing and increasing financial

---

19 J.W. Morris, *Memoirs of the Life and Writings of the Rev. Andrew Fuller* (London, 1816), 49.

20 On Thomas, see C.B. Lewis, *The Life of John Thomas* (London: Macmillan and Co., 1873); Arthur C. Chute, *John Thomas, First Baptist Missionary to Bengal, 1757–1801* (Halifax, Nova Scotia: Baptist Book and Tract Society, 1893).

indebtedness, as well as his mercurial temper. Thomas' dogmatic insistence on Calvinism and believer's baptism as requisite for participation in the Lord's Table was possibly the straw that broke the camel's back. As Thomas put it to Grant and other paedobaptists in Calcutta: "If the tiny pins of a watch are of so much value and use, notwithstanding their smallness, and if it be essential that they are rightly placed, who can say that the ordinances of God's house are less so."[21] Deep doctrinal convictions are vital, but the manner in which they are presented is also not unimportant. Carey would soon discern Thomas' dogmatic temperament on the voyage to India. As he wrote to Fuller about Thomas, "The more I know the more I love him—he is a very holy man—but his faithfulness often degenerates into personality."[22]

In time, Carey became aware that Grant was also not above blame in the disintegration of the relationship that forced Thomas, still deep in debt, to return to England in the early months of 1792 to secure funds to undergird his missionary work in Bengal.[23] Thomas also hoped to find, if at all possible, a like-minded companion for the work in India. Almost as soon as the ship had made landfall in England on July 8, Thomas got in touch with Samuel Stennett (1727–95) and Abraham Booth (1734–1806), two of the leading Baptist

---

21 Cited in Chute, *John Thomas*, 22.
22 William Carey to Andrew Fuller, October 23, 1793, in Leighton and Mornay Williams, eds., *Serampore Letters: Being the Unpublished Correspondence of William Carey and Others with John Williams* (New York: Fleming H. Revell, 1892), 37.
23 Chute, *John Thomas*, 26.

pastors in London. He made known to them his desire with regard to a mission to India. It was Booth who put Thomas into contact with Fuller and Carey. Thomas met up with these men in January 1793, and within a short period of time he and William Carey became the society's first appointees.

In Bengal, Thomas' instability of character and financial problems became a threat to the integrity of the mission. Despite this, Carey never ceased to be convinced that Thomas was "a man of great closet piety," very compassionate in his dealings with the poor in India, and indefatigable in teaching those who were seeking for truth.[24] And Fuller, for his part, had no doubt that Thomas' style of preaching was well suited to India: "a lively, metaphorical, and pointed address on divine subjects, dictated by the circumstances of the moment, and maintained amidst the interruptions and contradictions of a heathen audience."[25]

DOROTHY'S DEPRESSION AND MADNESS

But Carey faced an even more significant challenge before he ever set out to India: his wife, Dorothy, was utterly unwilling to go to India. She was persuaded to do so by Thomas when

---

24 William Carey to Andrew Fuller, November 1796, in Lewis, *Life of John Thomas*, 303.

25 Andrew Fuller, "Sketch of the Rev. John Thomas" in *The Last Remains of the Rev. Andrew Fuller: Sermons, Essays, Letters, and Other Miscellaneous Papers, Not Included in His Published Works* (Philadelphia: American Baptist Publication Society, 1856), 322–23.

he asked her younger sister Catharine Plackett if she would agree to go with Dorothy and her family to India. When Catherine said yes, Dorothy acceded. Dorothy's reluctance to support her husband has often been criticized, but it bears remembering that if she had ever traveled beyond her native Northamptonshire, it would only have been once or twice. Moreover, she had a very young family and was pregnant with a fourth child when they sailed to India. On the day she did agree to go, she spent time in prayer about the decision and was thus led to go with her husband.[26]

There is every indication she went with deep misgivings. Once in India, Dorothy began to lose her grip on reality when one of their sons, their third boy, Peter (1789–94), died at Mudnabati, near Dinajpur (now northern Bangladesh), where William had gone to be the manager of an indigo factory after their money soon ran out in Calcutta. None of the neighboring Hindus or Muslims would initially help the grieving family by acting as gravediggers, coffin makers, or even pallbearers, though eventually four Muslims did dig a grave for their son.[27] Over the next few years, Dorothy reached the point where she was completely delusional and believed that her husband was an unrepentant adulterer. She publicly accused him of such in quite vile terms and subsequently also made two attempts

---

26 Pearce Carey, *William Carey*, 130.

27 On the help of these Muslims, see William Carey to Samuel Pearce, January 29, [1795], in *Periodical Accounts Relative to the Baptist Missionary Society* (Clipston, England: J.W. Morris, 1800), I:127.

to kill him. By June 1800, William Ward simply stated in his diary, "Mrs. Carey is stark mad."[28]

Carey biographers have not been kind to Dorothy, and the way she has been treated in biographies of the Baptist leader are a fascinating study in their own right. Thankfully, James Beck, senior professor of counseling at Denver Seminary and a licensed clinical psychologist, had drawn up a very balanced account of Dorothy's life in his *Dorothy Carey: The Tragic and Untold Story of Mrs. William Carey*. This work's publication in 1992 coincided with the bicentennial of the formation of the Baptist Missionary Society. Beck's analysis in the book is judicious and balanced, especially given that Dorothy, illiterate when William married her, left not one scrap of written text. Attempting to draw a psychological portrait of her through the eyes of others is understandably difficult, and the danger of engaging in pure speculation enormous. Beck avoids this danger while at the same time producing an excellent psychological portrait of a very unhappy woman. Along the way, he raises important questions about areas of Carey's mission that need to be asked if an accurate account of Carey and the Serampore Mission is to be given. Beck does not question Carey's greatness but shows that, like the rest of us, he had feet of clay.

After Dorothy's death in 1807, Carey married two more times. In the summer of 1808 he and a Danish Christian by

---

28 Cited in James Beck, *Dorothy Carey: The Tragic and Untold Story of Mrs. William Carey* (Grand Rapids, Mich.: Baker, 1992), 152. For a helpful overview of Dorothy's loss of sanity, see Paul Pease, *Travel with William Carey* (Leominster: Day One Publications, 2005), 83–86.

the name of Charlotte Rumohr (1761–1821) married. He later remarked to one of his sons that "if he had searched the whole world, he could not have found a truer helpmate"— an allusion to Genesis 2 and the purpose of marriage—than in Charlotte.[29] Strong in faith, Charlotte was extremely frail, however, and died in 1821. A year later, Carey married Grace Hughes (1778–1835), who cared for the aged missionary in his final days.

LESSONS LEARNED AT MUDNABATI

Carey spent five years in the remote village of Mudnabati. Four things came out of this time of isolation and great trial. First, given the fact that there were next to no Europeans in the area, Carey was forced to acquire a remarkably extensive knowledge of Bengali. He also had time to begin learning Sanskrit, the classical language of the Indian subcontinent. Although Sanskrit was no longer a spoken language at the time when Carey was in India, Carey soon realized that Indians regarded this language as the only language worthy of literary production. It was a classical language that functioned much as Latin did in Europe during the Middle Ages. Carey realized that if the Bible were to be taken seriously by Indian religious leaders, it had to be translated into Sanskrit. Sanskrit was also the basis

---

29 Pearce Carey, *William Carey*, 292. For a brief account of her life, see Joseph Belcher, *William Carey: A Biography* (Philadelphia: American Baptist Publication Society, 1853), 259–66. See also Pearce Carey, *William Carey*, 292–94, 372–74.

for many other Indian languages, so Carey hoped that mastery of this language would make the task of translating the Scriptures into other languages easier.

Second, as soon as he had mastered elements of the Bengali language, Carey began work on the translation of the New Testament into Bengali, thus creating the dominant mold for his future ministry, namely, the translation of the Word of God. This Bengali New Testament, completed in 1797, would eventually progress through eight editions, each of them incorporating revisions and sometimes involving a complete retranslation.

It was also at Mudnabati that Carey's longstanding interest in botany began to flower (pun intended!). He began a garden and started researching ways to improve the agricultural lot of Bengali farmers, which would eventually result in Carey's becoming a leader in agricultural reform.[30] In Serampore, he had five acres or so under cultivation and continually asked his friends and correspondents to send him seeds, roots, and bulbs. For instance, in a letter to his close friend John Sutcliff in August 1809, Carey asked the English pastor to send him "a few tulips, daffodils, snowdrops, lilies." When Sutcliff dragged his feet about collecting them, Carey chided him:

Were you to give a penny a day to a boy to gather seeds of cowslips, violets, daisies, crowfoots, etc., and to dig

---

30 Franklyn J. Balasundaran, "Carey, William" in Scott W. Sunquist, ed., *A Dictionary of Asian Christianity* (Grand Rapids, Mich.: Eerdmans, 2001), 119.

up the roots of bluebells, etc., after they have done flowering, you might fill me a box each quarter of a year; and surely some neighbours would send a few snow-drops, crocuses, etc., and other trifles. All your weeds, even your nettles and thistles, are taken the greatest care of by me here. The American friends are twenty times more communicative than the English in this respect. . . . Do try to mend a little![31]

In time, Carey became an expert in the flora of Bengal and would be the main editor for William Roxburgh's *Hortus Bengalensis* (1814), which catalogued the plants in the East India Company's garden in Calcutta, as well as *Flora Indica* (1832), also by Roxburgh.[32]

Finally, Dorothy's illness forced him to develop a deeper trust in God. As Carey told his sisters in December 1796, "I am very fruitless and almost useless but the Word and the attributes of God are my hope, and my confidence, and my joy, and I trust that his glorious designs will undoubtedly be answered."[33]

---

31 William Carey to John Sutcliff, August 12, 1809, in Carey, *Memoir of William Carey*, 507.

32 For this area of Carey's life, see especially Keith Farrer, *William Carey: Missionary and Botanist* (Kew, Australia: Carey Baptist Grammar School, 2005), 75–110.

33 William Carey to Mary Carey and Ann Hobson, December 22, 1796, in *The Journal and Selected Letters of William Carey*, ed. Terry G. Carter (Macon, GA: Smyth & Helwys, 2000), 249.

The Friendship of Samuel Pearce

During the lonely days in Mudnabati, Carey drew solace from the letters that came from his friends, most of whom were in England. These letters usually took at least six months to reach India, but were received with much joy, and none more so than the correspondence from Samuel Pearce.

The Birmingham pastor attributed his missionary zeal to God's use of Carey's global passion. As he told Carey: "We lighted our torch at yours, and it was God who first touched your heart with fire from his holy altar. To Him be all the praise!"[34] This oneness of soul that Pearce and Carey had enjoyed in England prompted Carey to tell his friend a little before Carey sailed to India, "Well, you will come after us."[35] For a period of time in 1794, it looked like this might be the case, but Pearce was ever conscious that Christians are servants of a good master, the Lord Jesus, and it is he who ultimately determines where they should serve. As he told Carey:

> There is no part of my life which I reflect on with so much pleasure as that which has been spent in behalf of the society under whose patronage you are. And thrice happy should I be were the path of duty plain,

---

34 Samuel Pearce to William Carey, January 6, 1796, in *Missionary Correspondence: Containing Extracts of Letters from the Late Mr. Samuel Pearce, to the Missionaries in India, between the Years 1794, and 1798; and from Mr. John Thomas, from 1798, to 1800* (London: T. Gardiner and Son, 1814), 51–52.

35 Samuel Pearce to William Carey, October 24, 1794, in *Missionary Correspondence*, 19–20.

if I could personally share the toils and pleasures of the mission with you. At times I indulge a hope that my Lord will put me in a similar station; but then again I think, he well knows that I am inadequate to a task so arduous. Well, 'tis his to appoint; mine to acquiesce, submit, and obey. I trust, whenever or wherever he calls, I shall have grace immediately to say, "Speak, Lord, for thy servant heareth" [1 Sam. 3:9]. It is our mercy, my brother, that he chooses our inheritance for us. He knows best our fitness for the various posts in his spiritual kingdom; and so that we are but where he would have us and doing what he bids us, we may rejoice in the common hope that he will at last say to us all, "Well done" [Matt. 25:21, 23].[36]

In the midst of Carey's discouragements, Pearce sought, by means of his letters, to shine a ray of hope and light. As he told Carey on one occasion with reference to the preaching of the Moravians in Greenland:

Be not discouraged, my dear brother, if you do not succeed immediately. You know the [Moravian] Brethren laboured nearly six years without effect in Greenland; but they persevered, and now a tenth part of the inhabitants of that country are professors of the faith

---

36 Samuel Pearce to William Carey, August 9, 1794, in *Missionary Correspondence*, 12–13.

of Christ. But when I consider by what means they achieved so great a work, by the simple preaching of the cross of Christ and an exhibition of the love of his heart, I am constrained to say, "Not by might nor by power, but by thy Spirit, O Lord of Hosts" [Zech. 4:6]. I have lately been struck with a remark which applies to their labours and success. Facts interest more than speculations or abstract positions, however just. Talk to a child about any abstract subject and it requires pains to secure his attention; but tell him a story and he is all ear. So I should suppose an affectionate relation of the story of Jesus Christ, and his death and sufferings, would be the most likely way of engaging the heart of a heathen. But I, who am fifteen thousand miles from the seat of your labours, am almost ashamed to give my thoughts on a subject with which you must be so much better acquainted. Forgive my freedom and again believe me most affectionately yours in our dear Lord Jesus. [37]

This next letter, from 1796, similarly bespeaks the love that Pearce had for Carey, about which he was not afraid to speak openly:

O my dear brother, did you but know with what feelings I resume my pen, freely to correspond with you

---

37 Samuel Pearce to William Carey, August 27, 1795, in *Missionary Correspondence*, 49–50.

after receiving your very affectionate letter to myself and perusing that which you sent by the same conveyance to the Society, I am sure you would persuade yourself that I have no common friendship for you and that your regards are at least returned with equal ardour.

I fear (I had almost said) that I shall never see your face in the flesh; but if anything can add to the joy which the presence of Christ and conformity, perfect conformity, to him will afford in heaven, surely the certain prospect of meeting with my dear brother Carey there is one of the greatest.[38]

THE SERAMPORE TRIO

In late 1799, Carey moved with his family to Serampore, a Danish colony on the west bank of the Hooghly River a dozen or so miles from Calcutta. There he linked up with two new missionaries who had just arrived from England. William Ward was a printer whom Carey had met before he left England. He would become the best preacher at Serampore and would prove to be all but indispensable as the mission's "printing press manager, cross-cultural pastoral counselor, and peacemaker."[39] During his younger years, he had been

---

38 Samuel Pearce to William Carey, August 12, 1796, in Haykin, ed., *Memoirs of the Rev. Samuel Pearce*, 82.

39 A. Christopher Smith, "Ward, William," in Gerald H. Anderson, *Biographical Dictionary of Christian Missions* (Grand Rapids, Mich.: Eerdmans, 1998), 717. On Ward, see Samuel Stennett, *Memoir of the Life of the Rev. William Ward*, 2nd ed. (London, 1825); Marshman, *Life and Times of Carey, Marshman, and Ward*, 2 vols.;

involved in radical politics—it was, after all, a radical era, with revolutions in America and France. But he put this thirst for radical politics forever behind him when he went to India. Joshua Marshman was a man of tremendous diligence and blessed with an iron constitution. More pugnacious by nature than either Carey or Ward, Marshman easily assumed the role of apologist for the mission. Carey once described Marshman to Ryland as having "all eagerness for the work" of making Christ known in India. He had seen him, he told his English correspondent, seek to refute "men of lax conduct or deistical sentiments, and labor the point with them for hours together without fatigue." When it came to zeal, Carey felt he had to conclude, "he is a Luther and I am Erasmus."[40] Such zeal was needed at Serampore, for two Moravian missionaries, Karl Friedrich Schmidt and Johannes Grassman, had previously labored there from 1777 to 1792 but quit the field with the statement that preaching at Serampore was like plowing up a rock.[41]

A. Christopher Smith, "William Ward (1769–1823)," in Michael A.G. Haykin, ed., *The British Particular Baptists 1638–1910* (Springfield, Mo.: Particular Baptist, 2000), 2:255–71.

40 William Carey to John Ryland, May 24, 1810, cited in A. Christopher Smith, "Echoes of the Protestant Reformation in Baptist Serampore, 1800–1855," *The Baptist Review of Theology* 6, no. 1 (Spring 1996): 28–29. On Marshman, see Marshman, *Life and Times of Carey, Marshman, and Ward*, 2 vols.; A. Christopher Smith, "Joshua (1768–1837) and Hannah Marshman (1767–1847)," in Haykin, *The British Particular Baptists 1638–1910*, 2:237–53; Haykin, "The Legacy of the Senior Marshmans and William Ward," in *The Serampore Mission Enterprise* (Bangalore, India: Centre for Contemporary Christianity, 2006), 21–47.

41 Balasundaran, "Carey, William," 120.

So began the Serampore Mission, based around the partnership of these three men, a partnership that has few parallels in Christian history, and a work that, in the words of William Wilberforce, became "one of the chief glories of our country."[42] In all of the extant literature and manuscripts of these three men, there is amazingly no trace of mutual jealousy or severe anger. Henry Martyn (1781–1812), the evangelical Anglican and missionary to the Persians, who still needs a good solid biography, came for a five-month stay at Serampore in 1806. And what Carey noted of his stay with them bespeaks the sort of ambience that permeated the relationships between himself and Ward and Marshman: "As the image or shadow of bigotry is not known among us here, we take sweet counsel together, and go to the house of God as friends."[43]

CAREY THE TRANSLATOR

Carey's principal contribution to the Serampore Mission was through his remarkable linguistic ability. As we have noted, by the time that Carey moved to Serampore, he had acquired an extensive knowledge of both Bengali and Sanskrit. The Bengali New Testament was completely published by February 1801. Seven years later, the New Testament in Sanskrit was being seen through the press. All told, Carey translated

---

42 E. Daniel Potts, *British Baptist Missionaries in India, 1793–1837* (Cambridge, England: Cambridge University Press, 1967), 17.

43 Cited in Stephen Neill, *A History of Christian Missions* (Harmondsworth, England: Penguin, 1964), 266.

or supervised the translation of the Scriptures into six of the great languages of India—Bengali, Sanskrit, Marathi, Hindi, Assamese, and Oriya—as well as parts of the Scriptures into twenty-nine other languages.[44] In these early years of the modern missionary movement, 43 percent of first translations of the Scriptures into new languages anywhere in the world were published at Serampore. India has more than 120 major languages with hundreds of minor ones, so this may seem but a drop in the bucket, but it was a remarkable achievement.[45]

As a grammarian, Carey was brilliant. As a translator, though, it must be admitted that he lacked "a keen sensitiveness to the finer shades and nuances of ideas and meaning," a failing that dogged all of his translations.[46] Carey remarked frequently that he knew the translations were not perfect and he hoped that others would build on them. Carey believed that a translation should be geared as much as possible to the grammatical structure and wording of the original Hebrew or Greek. But in following this principle, he failed to make the Scriptures communicate in the living language of the people of India. It is not fortuitous that the translation that survived the longest was his translation into Sanskrit. It was thirty-three years before it was replaced with a new translation. Perhaps it

---

44 B. Stanley, "Carey, William" in Timothy Larsen, et al., eds., *Biographical Dictionary of Evangelicals* (Leicester, England: Inter-Varsity Press, 2003), 120.

45 Norman Davies, *Beneath Another Sky: A Global Journey into History* ([London]: Allen Lane, 2017), 144.

46 Stephen Neill, *A History of Christianity in India 1707–1858* (Cambridge, England: Cambridge University Press, 1985), 190.

lasted longer because it was a classical, written language and not a spoken, vernacular language. It needs to be noted that Carey's failure to understand at times the subtleties of translation was a common failing of the day among translators. A good exception is Adoniram Judson's (1788–1850) translation of the Scriptures into Burmese. His Burmese Bible is still in use and has remained readable, whereas none of Carey's translations are still being used.

Driving Carey, though, was the deep conviction that the Word of God had to be available to the various peoples that he was trying to reach. He was rightly convinced that the Word of God is in itself the great instrument for the conversion of unbelievers. And yet, he would have probably achieved more if he had attempted less.

CHAPTER FIVE

The Serampore Mission

Up until the move to Serampore, Carey had not seen any lasting spiritual fruit among the Indian people. Within a year of the start of the mission at Serampore, however, converts began to come in. The first was Krishna Pal (1764–1822), a Hindu carpenter and longtime seeker after truth.

KRISHNA PAL

Pal had heard the gospel already from one of the Moravian missionaries who had labored in the vicinity of Serampore, but it had made no lasting impression on his mind. On the morning of November 25, 1800, however, while he was washing in the Hooghly River, not far from the Serampore Mission, he fell on the slippery bank and dislocated his shoulder. He sought help from John Thomas, who came to his home with Marshman and Carey. Thomas set his arm, and the three missionaries shared some Scripture with Pal. That evening, Thomas and Marshman returned and gave Pal this rhyme to ponder along with a full explanation of its meaning (Pal was used to such forms of wording since mantras played a large role in his Hindu convictions):

Sin confessing, sin forsaking,
Christ's righteousness embracing,
The soul is free.[1]

A month or so later, Krishna Pal told Thomas that he believed that "Christ gave his life up for the salvation of sinners" and that he had personally embraced this gospel truth. He subsequently broke caste by eating with the missionaries, and Ward commented rightly: "The door of faith is open to the Gentiles; who shall shut it? The chain of the caste is broken, who shall mend it?"[2] On Sunday, December 28, 1800, a few days after his profession of faith and in the presence of a huge crowd of Europeans, Hindus, and Muslims, he was baptized by Carey in the Hooghly River.[3]

Sadly, John Thomas suffered a major mental breakdown around the time of Pal's baptism and by October of that year

---

1   *The First Hindoo Convert: A Memoir of Krishna Pal* (Philadelphia: American Baptist Publication Society, 1852), 9–11.

2   .Cited in "Memoir of the Rev. William Ward," *New Evangelical Magazine and Theological Review* 10 (1824): 3.

3   *First Hindoo Convert*, 14–17.

lay dying at the home of Ignatius Fernandez (1757–1831), a Portuguese convert. It is fitting to remember Thomas, though. He was not without his failings, and he did not prove to be the friend that Carey needed during his first years in India. But his deep love for the Indian people and his hunger for their conversion should never be forgotten.

Pal was the first of hundreds who were converted through the witness of the Serampore Mission over the next three decades. By 1821, more than 1,400 believers—half of them Indians—had been baptized, and Krishna Pal, who died the following year, had become one of the finest preachers of the Serampore Mission. Carey once described an early sermon of this Indian brother as "fluent, perspicuous, and affectionate, in a very high degree."[4] And in 1811, Carey told John Sutcliff in a letter that Pal was a "zealous, well-informed, and I may add, eloquent minister of the gospel," who was regularly preaching twelve to fourteen times a week in Calcutta or its environs.[5]

Pal also wrote hymns to express his love, and that of his fellow Bengali believers, for Christ. One of them, translated into English, is still in use in certain evangelical circles. Its first stanza runs thus:

O thou, my soul, forget no more,
The Friend who all thy misery bore;

---

4   Cited in *First Hindoo Convert*, 38.
5   Cited in *First Hindoo Convert*, 67.

Let every idol be forgot,
But, O my soul, forget him not.[6]

In its cross-centeredness and with its focus on the power of the cross to deliver from idolatry, this verse is quintessentially evangelical and well captures the heart of why Carey and his colleagues were in India. The description of the Lord Jesus Christ as the "Friend who all thy misery bore" is striking in view of the fact that at the heart of the Serampore Mission were the bonds between the three friends Carey, Marshman, and Ward.

There are some today who view the Serampore Trio and their colleagues primarily as social reformers—since they helped abolish such social ills as *sati* (the self-immolation of a widow on the funeral pyre of her husband) and the prostitution of children in the Hindu temples—and educational activists. Indeed, their founding of Serampore College in 1818 to provide an education irrespective of caste or ethnicity and train men for ministry in India was a remarkable achievement. But this would be to confuse the root of their ministry with its fruit. Sending forth the gospel with its message of the crucified Christ whose death alone delivers from sin and its consequences was the main thing these men and women were

---

6   See *Grace Hymns* (London: Grace Publications Trust, 1975), Hymn 145, stanza 1. For a study of the hymn, see David W. Music, "Krishna Pal's 'O Thou, My Soul, Forget No More' and 'Global Hymnody' among Nineteenth-Century Baptists," *American Baptist Quarterly* 28 (2009): 194–207. Music argues that Joshua Marshman, who translated the hymn into English, has reshaped elements of it to reflect a profounder theology.

about. The social and educational impact of that proclamation was a happy byproduct of their gospel preaching. To view these men primarily as social reformers is to do them a grave injustice.

SERAMPORE FORM OF AGREEMENT (1805)

The core principles by which Carey, Marshman, and Ward operated the mission can be found in the Serampore Form of Agreement, drawn up in 1805. A brief review of this text is vital to understanding the heart of this Christian mission.[7]

First of all, Carey and his colleagues expressed their conviction that the non-Christian peoples of India had to be valued for what they were—immortal souls, but men and women who had no true knowledge of their Maker. As the Serampore missionaries wrote:

> In order to be prepared for our great and solemn work, it is absolutely necessary that we set an infinite value upon immortal souls; that we often endeavor to affect our minds with the dreadful loss sustained by an unconverted soul launched into eternity. It becomes us to fix in our minds the awful doctrine of eternal punishment, and to realize frequently the

---

7 For the full text, see Appendix 3: The Serampore Form of Agreement (1805). There is good evidence to indicate that William Ward actually drafted this covenantal text, but Carey and the other Serampore missionaries signed it, and thereby indicated their full agreement with its contents.

inconceivably awful condition of this vast country, lying in the arms of the wicked one. If we have not his awful sense of the value of souls, it is impossible that we can feel aright in any other part of our work, and in this case it had been better for us to have been in any other situation rather than in that of a missionary. Oh! may our hearts bleed over these poor idolaters, and may their case lie with continued weight on our minds, that we may resemble that eminent mission-ary, who compared the travail of his soul, on account of the spiritual state of those committed to his charge, to the pains of childbirth.[8]

The "eminent Missionary" in view here is obviously the Apostle Paul, and the biblical text being alluded to is Galatians 4:19. The Serampore text went on to express the hope that, if God could plant saving truth among "the sottish and bru-talized Britons," he could just as easily do the same in India. The British missionaries were thus confident that God would eventually "famish all the gods of India" and cause idolaters in the Indian subcontinent "to cast their idols to the moles and to the bats, and renounce for ever the work of their own hands."[9]

Second, in order for the missionaries to best reach the various people groups of India, each people group had to be

---

8   Serampore Form of Agreement 1.
9   Serampore Form of Agreement 1.

approached in its own language. This entailed each mission-ary's learning the local language of the people that he was trying to reach. This was a fundamental principle of Carey's mission, and it was the impetus behind the attempt referred to above to make the Scriptures available in as many tongues of India as possible.[10] Linked to this translation project was also a commitment to become deeply familiar with the "modes of thinking, . . . habits, . . . propensities, . . . [and] antipathies" of the Indian people.[11] One of the ways that Carey sought to do this was by printing various Indian texts that best exempli-fied the worldview of the Indian people. Not surprisingly, this caused some concern back home in England, but Carey was adamant that this was needed to understand why the Indians thought the way that they did.[12]

Third, although Carey and his colleagues were not averse to pointing out to their Indian hearers what they judged to be the weaknesses and imperfections of Hinduism and Islam, they did not begin with such a critique. As the Serampore Form of Agreement put it: "Nor is it advisable at once to attack their prejudices by exhibiting with acrimony the sins of their gods; neither should we upon any account do violence to their images, nor interrupt their worship: the real conquests of the gospel are those of love: 'And I, if I be lifted up, will

10 See also Serampore Form of Agreement 9.
11 Serampore Form of Agreement 2.
12 Stephen Neill, *A History of Christianity in India 1707–1858* (Cambridge, England: Cambridge University Press, 1985), 191–92, 504n20.

draw all men unto me' [John 12:32]."[13] As far as possible, they sought to avoid giving offense to non-Christians: "Those parts of English manners which are most offensive to them should be kept out of sight as much as possible. We should also avoid every degree of cruelty to animals."[14] The latter remark was, of course, necessary in a Hindu context where numerous animals were the object of devotion.[15]

Fourth, Carey and his friends were determined to place Christ crucified at the heart of their preaching. They were convinced that this was Paul's methodology, for the "doctrine of Christ's expiatory death and all-sufficient merits has been, and must ever remain, the grand means of conversion." Proof of the efficacy of this type of preaching was found in the fact that the cross was central to the preaching of the Reformers and that of such eighteenth-century evangelists as George Whitefield. The Serampore missionaries had also found that "the astonishing and all-constraining love exhibited in our

---

13 Serampore Form of Agreement 3. The one striking exception to this principle took place when a booklet deeply critical of Muhammad, known to history as *The Persian Pamphlet*, was printed in 1807 by the Serampore Press after Ward had given it only a cursory reading. See Peter Morden, "Andrew Fuller as an Apologist for Missions" in Michael A.G. Haykin, ed., *"At the Pure Fountain of Thy Word": Andrew Fuller as an Apologist* (Milton Keyes, England: Paternoster, 2004), 247–48.

14 Serampore Form of Agreement 3.

15 The deep interest Carey had in botany has been noted above. He was also fascinated by the animal world. Carey saw in the animal world incontestable proof of "the wisdom and goodness of the universal Parent of all creatures." Study of the various animals should ultimately "raise the mind to sublime meditation upon and admiration of their Maker." See William Carey, "On the Study of Nature," *The Friend of India* (Monthly Series) 8 (1825): 247–50.

Redeemer's propitiatory death" was foremost in the conversion of every Hindu to that point in time through their mission.[16]

While baptism was not long delayed for new converts, it was to be followed by a period of Christian instruction and nurture.[17] Nor was it necessary to change the names of Indian converts so as to replace their names with biblical ones. Thus, the first convert, Krishna Pal, had been named after a Hindu deity, but he retained his name after his conversion.[18] On the other hand, conversion did entail a renunciation of caste and the caste system. By eating with the missionaries and the other native believers, whatever their social background, new converts demonstrated the reality of their desire to be part of the Christian family.[19]

Fifth, every encouragement was to be given to Indian believers to develop their gifts with the confidence that some of them would become preachers, for, the Serampore missionaries believed, "it is only by means of native preachers that we can hope for the universal spread of the Gospel throughout this immense continent."[20] This in turn would soon lead to the founding of Indian churches pastored by Indian brethren, who, in due course, would send out missionaries to the four corners of the subcontinent.[21] As an

---

16 Serampore Form of Agreement 5.

17 Serampore Form of Agreement 7.

18 Serampore Form of Agreement 8.

19 See the comments of Neill, *History of Christianity in India*, 198.

20 Serampore Form of Agreement 8.

21 Serampore Form of Agreement 8.

autodidact, Carey especially knew the value of knowledge, and the Serampore covenant emphasized that in "preparing the Hindoos for casting their idols to the moles and the bats," it was essential to have native schools to give future pastors and missionaries an elementary education.[22] Within a few years, the missionaries had established a hundred or so of these schools.[23] And in 1818, they started Serampore College as primarily a divinity school for leaders and pastors, though non-Christians could also pursue studies there. By the time of Carey's death sixteen years later, the college had more than eighty students.[24]

Finally, the Serampore Form of Agreement stressed the need for prayer to undergird the entirety of the mission. It is "secret, fervent, believing prayer"—what Carey could also call "a heart given up to God in closet religion"—that is essential to both a holy life and a useful life in God's "great work of human redemption."[25] Surely the fact that the Baptist Missionary Society had been born in prayer and that Carey had seen the beginnings of the impact of corporate prayer meetings for revival in England lay behind this emphasis on prayer.

---

22 Serampore Form of Agreement 9. See the detailed argument about this point in William Carey, Joshua Marshman, and William Ward, *College for the Instruction of Asiatic Christian and Other Youth, in Eastern Literature and European Science, at Serampore, Bengal* (London: Black, Kingsbury, Parbury, and Allen, 1819), 1–6.

23 Neill, *History of Christianity in India*, 199–200.

24 Neill, *History of Christianity in India*, 200–201.

25 Serampore Form of Agreement 10.

THE LOSS OF ENGLISH FRIENDS
AND THE IMPACT AT SERAMPORE[26]

By the time that the Serampore Form of Agreement was drawn up, Carey's good friend Samuel Pearce had died. Within ten years, two other English friends had also passed away: Sutcliff and Fuller. Carey especially felt Fuller's death in 1815 keenly. When he heard of it, he wrote to Ryland: "I loved him. . . . There was scarcely any other man in England to whom I could so completely lay open my heart."[27] Since the founding of the society in 1792, Fuller had been Carey's closest friend and champion. Of their intimate association, John Clark Marshman wrote:

> The connection between the three missionaries at Serampore and Mr. Fuller was characterized by that identity of feeling which seems to belong peculiarly to the early stages of a great undertaking, when congenial minds are absorbed in removing the obstacles which impede the prosecution of it. They began the enterprise together, and they pursued it with unbroken unanimity. Though separated from each other by the distance of half the globe, they appeared to

---

26 I am deeply indebted to my doctoral student Matthew M. Reynolds, who is writing his doctoral dissertation on William Ward, for help with the writing of this section on the conflict between the Serampore Mission and the Baptist Missionary Society in London.

27 S. Pearce Carey, *William Carey*, 8th ed. (London: Carey, 1934), 334.

be intuitively acquainted with each other's thoughts and feelings, and their mutual communications were marked by the total absence of any feeling of reserve. The three men at Serampore were prepared to yield without servility to the judgment of their associates in England, and this feeling was fully reciprocated by Mr. Fuller and his two colleagues [i.e., John Sutcliff and John Ryland]. It was not a time for the nice adjustment of the boundaries of authority, and there was never any suspicion that either party would encroach on the province or the independence of the other.[28]

Marshman's mention of there being no "feeling of reserve" between these friends can be illustrated by a snippet of a letter that Fuller sent to Carey after the latter had asked Fuller to adhere to the way he spelled Indian words. To this Fuller replied:

But you do not always spell alike. Sometimes you write *moonshee*, and sometimes *munshi*.[29] If the trumpet give an uncertain sound, who can prepare for the battle? You must again allow me to remind you of your punctuation. I never knew a person of so much knowledge as you possess of other languages, write English so bad! You huddle half-a-dozen periods into

---

28 John Clark Marshman, *The Life and Times of Carey, Marshman, and Ward* (1859; repr., Serampore, India: Council of Serampore College, 2005), 2:103.

29 *Munshi* is a Persian loanword that was used for native language teachers in the Mughal Empire and British India.

one. Where your sentence ends, you very commonly make only a semicolon, instead of a period. If your Bengali New Testament should be thus pointed, I should tremble for its fate.[30]

But though such unquestioned trust was the norm between Fuller and the Serampore Trio, Fuller was well aware of those within the Baptist Missionary Society who wanted to move in a different direction. Some of the younger members of the society wanted to put all of the society's missionaries on salary (as other missionary societies were beginning to do) and manage their affairs from London. Fuller foresaw the consternation this would cause in Serampore and said as much in a letter he wrote to the trio two years before his death:

If ever the committee begins to legislate for India, I should expect they [Serampore] would issue a declaration of independence, and I should not be sorry if they did. We have never pretended to govern them, for two reasons. One is, we think them better able to govern themselves, than we are to govern them; another is, they are at far too great a distance to await our directions. Our business has been little more than to furnish them, as far as we were able, with means, and to send out a few recruits.[31]

---

30 Cited in Arthur C. Chute, *John Thomas, First Baptist Missionary to Bengal, 1757–1801* (Halifax, Nova Scotia: Baptist Book and Tract Society, 1893), 21n*.

31 Cited in Marshman, *Life and Times of Carey, Marshman, and Ward*, 2:79.

When Fuller died in the spring of 1815, John Ryland, the only surviving founding member of the society, was appointed secretary in Fuller's place, but he was quickly caught between the rock of his longstanding friendship with the Serampore brethren and the hard place of younger men in the society who didn't know the trio and who desired to seize the reins of the society.[32] Like Fuller, Ryland understood the implicit trust upon which the relationship between the leadership of the society and the Serampore Mission had been based. But he also understood that the younger members of the society had exacting questions that those in Serampore might have difficulty answering, such as: "When were the premises at first purchased? In whose names, and with what money? . . . If they stand in your names already, can you make them over to yourselves in trust? . . . May not their heirs take possession after them, and should we not find it difficult to turn them out?"[33]

Such questions had never been asked by Fuller or his close friends. But they were the type of exacting, legal questions that prompted a decades-long controversy between the Baptist Missionary Society in London and the Serampore Mission in India. In short, the London head office wanted control of the mission premises and the affairs of the Serampore Mission. Carey and his friends were willing to concede the property but not the control of it. They would allow the Baptist Missionary Society to own it, provided they as seniors in the mission be

---

32 Marshman, *Life and Times of Carey, Marshman, and Ward*, 2:135.
33 Marshman, *Life and Times of Carey, Marshman, and Ward*, 2:138.

allowed to continue as trustees for life.[34] Soon their incomes, standard of living, and even modes of transportation came under intense scrutiny.[35] Voluminous correspondence passed back and forth over the Indian and Atlantic oceans attempting to clarify each side's position and reach an amicable settlement. Both Ward and Marshman, on separate occasions, went back to England, where they devoted much time to seeking to repair the breach, but the end result was that Marshman's character was greatly sullied.

The pamphlets from both sides in this sad struggle would eventually fill two bulky volumes.[36] The Baptist Missionary Society and the Serampore Mission parted ways and only reunited just before Marshman's death in 1837, although he died before the happy news of this reunion reached Serampore.[37] This sad saga really needs a thorough study, but in the light of this study of friendship, it powerfully illustrates the way that Christian missions and institutions can go sadly astray when friendship is not at the heart of them.

CAREY'S FINAL YEARS

In his final years, Carey became increasingly vocal in his writings about his only plea for acceptance with God: the shed

---

34 Marshman, *Life and Times of Carey, Marshman, and Ward*, 2:146–47.

35 Marshman, *Life and Times of Carey, Marshman, and Ward*, 2:178–81.

36 Marshman, *Life and Times of Carey, Marshman, and Ward*, 2:381.

37 Marshman, *Life and Times of Carey, Marshman, and Ward*, 2:510–11, 345–46.

blood of Jesus Christ for his sins. In a letter that he wrote on May 17, 1831, he told his son Jabez:

> I am this day seventy years old—a monument of divine mercy and goodness; though, on a review of my life, I find much, very much, for which I ought to be humbled in the dust. My direct and positive sins are innumerable; my negligence in the Lord's work has been great; I have not promoted his cause nor sought his glory and honor as I ought. Notwithstanding all this, I am spared till now and am still retained in his work. I trust for acceptance with him to the blood of Christ alone; and I hope I am received into the divine favor through him. I wish to be more entirely devoted to his service, more completely sanctified, and more habitually exercising all the Christian graces, and bringing forth the fruits of righteousness to the praise and honor of that Savior who gave his life a sacrifice for sin.[38]

Here are two theological themes that were foundational to the entirety of Carey's thought and mission that have been sketched above. First, the death of Christ for sinners is the Christian's only plea with regard to salvation when he stands in the presence of a holy God at the final judgment. Second,

---

38 Eustace Carey, *Memoir of William Carey, D.D.* (London: Jackson and Walford, 1836), 566–67.

the ultimate goal of the Christian life is the glory of God. Carey felt that he had not made the latter uppermost throughout his life; hence his comfort in the former.

Similar thoughts fill another letter that Carey wrote in 1831, this one to his sisters in England. John Webster Morris, whom Carey had known many years earlier, was hoping to write something about Carey to satisfy a British public clamoring for details about the life of the Baptist missionary. Carey had clearly become something of a celebrity. Carey wanted nothing to do with such "celebrification." As he told his sisters:

> Dear Morris wrote to me for letters and other documents to assist him in writing memoirs of me after my death, but there was a spirit in his letter which I must disapprove. I therefore told him so in my reply, and absolutely refused to send anything. Indeed I have no wish that anyone should write or say anything about me; let my memorial sleep with my body in the dust and at the last great day all the good or evil which belongs to my character will be fully known. My great concern now is to be found in Christ. His atoning sacrifice is all my hope; and I know that sacrifice to be of such value that God has accepted it as fully vindicating his government in the exercise of mercy to sinners and as that on account of which he will accept the greatest offender who seeks to him for pardon. And the acceptance of that sacrifice of atonement

was testified by the resurrection of our Lord from the dead and by the commission to preach the gospel to all nations, with a promise or rather a declaration that whosoever believeth on the Son shall be saved, "shall not come into condemnation but is passed from death unto life" [John 5:24].[39]

Given such sentiments, it is not surprising that Carey gave explicit instructions that apart from his date of birth and death, nothing was to be inscribed upon his tombstone but these words from a hymn of Isaac Watts: "A wretched, poor, and helpless worm, On Thy kind arms I fall."[40]

ROPEHOLDERS

When Carey's circle of friends—Fuller, Sutcliff, Ryland, and Pearce—were contemplating the mission that sent Carey to India in 1793, one of the images that kept coming to their minds was that of a deep mine. As Andrew Fuller later recalled in a letter to Christopher Anderson:

Our undertaking to India really appeared at its beginning to me somewhat like a few men, who were deliberating about the importance of penetrating a

---

39 Cited in Ernest A. Payne, "A 'Carey' Letter of 1831," *The Baptist Quarterly* 9 (1938–39): 240–41.

40 Carey, *Memoir of William Carey*, 572–73.

deep mine, which had never before been explored. We had no one to guide us; and whilst we were thus deliberating, Carey, as it were, said, "Well, I will go down, if you will hold the rope." But, before he descended, he, as it seemed to me, took an oath from each of us at the mouth of the pit, to this effect that "whilst we lived, we should never let go the rope."[41]

As we have seen, the response of Fuller, Sutcliff, Ryland, and Pearce was wholehearted, earnest, and undertaken out of a fervent passion for God's glory and a deep love for Carey.

One final comment: the commitment of these men to one another is well summed up in the words that Samuel Pearce wrote in the front of a Greek New Testament that he sent to Carey in the autumn of 1797. In choosing these particular words, Pearce was obviously seeking to remind Carey what God had done for them by joining them together in Christian friendship. Appropriately, five of them were in Greek and were drawn from Acts 4:32: "A small token of the great esteem he bears his dear brother Carey. . . . καρδια και ψθχη μια [one heart and one soul]."[42]

41 Pearce Carey, *William Carey*, 118.
42 John Taylor, ed., *Biographical and Literary Notices of William Carey, D.D.* (Northampton, England: The Dryden Press, Taylor & Son, 1886), 27.

ACKNOWLEDGMENTS

A select number of sections of this book appeared as monthly installments throughout 2011 in the magazine *The Gospel Witness*, which is published by Jarvis Street Baptist Church, Toronto. These are used by permission. Sections of this book have also been adapted from my *One Heart and One Soul: John Sutcliff of Olney, His Friends, and His Times* (Darlington, England: Evangelical, 1994), which is now out of print.

And it is fitting, in a book about friendship, to extend my gratitude for help freely offered by the following friends: Chisso Wang, for drawing up the timeline of Carey's life; Sam Masters, for answers to various queries; Paul Gillespie, for research; Grant Gordon, for access to his essay on Newton's impact on Carey; and Matthew M. Reynolds, for help with the subsection of chapter 5 dealing with the rift between the Baptist Missionary Society and the Serampore Trio.

—Michael A.G. Haykin
Dundas, Ontario
January 29, 2018

A TIMELINE OF
WILLIAM CAREY'S LIFE

1756	Dorothy Plackett, Carey's first wife, born in Piddington, Northamptonshire
1761, Aug 17	William Carey born to Edmund and Elizabeth Carey in a small cottage in Pury End near Paulerspury, Northamptonshire
1763	Carey's sister Ann born
1767	Edmund (father) appointed as schoolmaster to Paulerspury School House. Family moves from Pury End to Paulerspury; sister Mary born
1773	John Wesley visits Northamptonshire; Carey finishes school
1775	Carey sent to Clarke Nichols of Piddington to be apprenticed as a shoemaker and meets fellow apprentice, John Warr
1779, Feb 10	George III proclaims national day of prayer in regard to the American Revolution. Carey invited by Warr to go to the Dissenters' Meetinghouse in Hackleton. Thomas Chater

	preaches, and Carey becomes convinced that he should leave the Anglican Church
1779, Sept	Carey's master, Clarke Nichols, dies
1779, Oct 5	Carey accepted as a journeyman to Thomas Old
1779–82	Carey meets mystics from Quinton that cause him to struggle with assurance for three years
1781, Jun 10	Carey marries Dorothy Plackett, Thomas Old's sister-in-law
1781	Carey preaches first sermon at Hackleton meetinghouse
1782	Preaches to a Dissenting congregation in Earls Barton
1782	First child, Ann (named after Carey's grandmother), born
1783	Carey's sisters, Ann and Mary, baptized by Thomas Skinner
1783, Oct 5	Carey baptized by John Ryland Jr.
1784	Carey's daughter Ann dies
1785, Mar 25	Moves to Moulton and opens a school. Occasionally preaches at Moulton Baptist Church
1785	Felix Carey born
1787, Aug 1	Ordained minister at Moulton Baptist Church. Andrew Fuller, John Ryland Jr., and John Sutcliff participate in the service

1787	Dorothy Carey baptized
1788	William Carey Jr. born
1789, Feb	Carey asked by Harvey Lane Church in Leicester to be their pastor
1789, Jun	Accepts call to be the pastor at Harvey Lane Church
1789	Peter Carey born
1790 Sept	Dissolves Harvey Lane Church and reforms it on the basis of the Leicester Church Covenant
1791, May 24	Formally ordained as the pastor of Harvey Lane Baptist Church
1791	Lucy Carey born
1792, May	*The Enquiry* published
1792, May 30	Preaches at the Northamptonshire Association Meeting in Nottingham from Isaiah 54:2–3
1792, Oct 2	Baptist Missionary Society birthed in Kettering
1793	Jabez Carey born
1793, Jan 9	Meets John Thomas
1793, Mar 31	Meets William Ward at Carter Lane Chapel
1793, Jun 13	Sets sail from Dover to India with family
1793, Nov 11	Arrives in India
1794, summer	Moves to Mudnabati to manage Indigo factory
1794, Oct	Peter Carey dies

1796, Jan	Jonathan Carey born
1797	Translation of Bengali New Testament completed
1799, Oct	William Ward, Joshua and Hannah Marshman arrive
1800, Jan 10	Carey and family move to Serampore and establish a missionary community
1800, Dec 28	First Bengali convert, Krishna Pal, baptized as well as Carey's son Felix
1801, Feb	First Bengali New Testament printed by Serampore Press
1801, Apr	Carey appointed teacher at Fort William College, Calcutta
1801, Oct	John Thomas dies
1807	Felix Carey ordained
1807	Carey awarded doctorate by Brown University
1807, Dec 8	Dorothy Carey dies
1808, May 9	Marries Charlotte Rumohr (1761–1821)
1808	Sanskrit New Testament published
1812, Mar 11	Fire destroys the printing house; years of translation work lost
1814, Jun 22	John Sutcliff dies
1815, May 7	Andrew Fuller dies
1815	Tension between Baptist Missionary Society and Serampore Mission begins
1818	Serampore College founded

1818	Sanskrit Bible published
1820, Sept 14	Agricultural Society of Bengal organized
1821, May 30	Charlotte, Carey's second wife, dies
1822, July 22	Carey marries Grace Hughes (1778–1835)
1822, Aug	Krishna Pal dies
1822, Nov 10	Felix, Carey's son, dies
1823, Mar 7	William Ward dies of cholera
1825, May 25	John Ryland Jr. dies
1827, Mar 17	Serampore Mission severs ties with Baptist Missionary Society
1829	Sati abolished
1834, Jun 9	Carey dies at sunrise at Serampore
1835, Jul 27	Grace, Carey's third wife, dies
1837, Dec 5	Joshua Marshman dies

THE LEICESTER COVENANT
(1790)[1]

We, the Church of Jesus Christ meeting in Harvey Lane, Leicester, being convinced of the importance of impartial discipline and pure doctrine in order to our peace and prosperity in the ways of God, do in the presence of God, and of one another, solemnly covenant and agree, in manner and form as follows:

I. That we receive the Bible as the Word of God, and the only rule of faith, and practice, in which we find the following doctrines taught, namely, that in the Deity are three equal persons, the Father, the Son, and the Holy Spirit, who sustain distinct offices in the economy of human salvation; We believe that all things were fully known to God from the foundation of the world, that he from eternity chose his people in Christ to salvation through sanctification of the Spirit and belief of

---

1 From John Appleby, *"I Can Plod . . ." William Carey and the Early Years of the First Baptist Missionary Society* (London: Grace, 2007), 285–87. Appleby transcribed it from a photocopy of the original church minute book held in the Record Office for Leicestershire, Leicester & Rutland, Wigston Magna, Leicester. The spelling and punctuation have been modernized.

the truth; that all rational creatures are under indispensable obligation to obey the Law of God, which is holy, just and good, but that all men have broken it and are liable to eternal punishment; that in the fullness of time God sent his Son to redeem his people whose blood was a sufficient atonement for sin, and by the imputation of whose righteousness we are accounted righteous before God, and accepted with him; and that being justified by faith we have peace with God through our Lord Jesus Christ. We further believe that men are totally depraved, and that the carnal mind is enmity against God, and that we are convicted, and converted only by the sovereign operations of the Holy Spirit upon our hearts, being made willing in the day of his power, and that the life of Grace is maintained by the same Divine Spirit, who is the finisher as well as the author of our faith, that those who are received thus shall persevere in the way of holiness, and at last obtain everlasting happiness through the mercy of God.

II. That we will pay the strictest regard to our conduct in the world, acting with the strictest honesty and integrity in all our worldly dealings, we will likewise abstain from all unlawful amusements and diversions by which time would be wasted, money spent, our minds carnalized, our brethren's minds hurt, or religion dishonored. We will abstain from worldly labor on the Lord's Day, and carefully sanctify it, we will pay the strictest regard to our promises, and by an holy conduct endeavor to honor the cause of God.

III. Also that we will endeavor to train up our families in the fear of the Lord, and to instruct and govern our households as little charges entrusted to us.

IV. That we consistently attend the worship of God on Sundays, at Church Meetings, and other meetings appointed by the Church; if we ever are absent we will be ready to give a reason why, if required; if we are absent from public worship three Sabbaths, or should attend but only in three weeks for six weeks together, or if we are once absent from the Lord's Supper or twice from Church Meetings without just cause, it should be a sufficient reason why the Church should visit and enquire the reason, and deal accordingly, as shall be required. At our Church meetings only one of our brethren shall speak at a time, and if in any matter a difference should take place, we will endeavor to weigh the matter deliberately and fully, and then put it to the Vote that it may be determined by the majority to which the majority shall peacefully accede; all our sisters shall have the same right to vote as the brethren, and be as capable of giving evidence in any matter; yet they shall not be permitted to dictate. We will not watch for each other's faults but will visit each other, mourning with the mourners and joining in the joy of them that rejoice; we will warn, rebuke, exhort, and encourage with long suffering, and desire to keep the unity of the Spirit in the bond of peace. If called to act against those who break the Law of our Lord's house we will do it in the spirit of the Gospel, admonishing, suspending, or excluding, as the matter of the case requires.

V. We will regard and highly esteem our minister for his work's sake, constantly attending on his ministry and freely consulting him on the concern of our souls, contributing according to our ability to his comfortable support, and avoiding all that may weaken his hands, or discourage his mind; in a word we will all seek the good of the Body with which we are connected and if the good of the Body calls us to sacrifice our own case or interest, we will cheerfully do it; esteeming the honor of Christ as far preferable to our own.

VI. We will seek out those in our congregation who appear under concern of soul, and having good evidence of a work of grace on their hearts, will set before them the Privileges they have a right to, and the duties they ought to be found in, and endeavor to remove the stumbling blocks out of their way that they may enjoy the communion of saints.

VII. To receive such, and only such into our communion who make a credible profession of repentance towards God, and faith in our Lord Jesus Christ, and who have been baptized according to the primitive mode of administering that ordinance, that is, by immersing them in water, in the name of the Father, the Son, and the Holy Spirit.

VIII. That in all personal misunderstandings the person offended shall go to the offender, and in a spirit of love seek to be reconciled, before the matter be reported to any other. That all debates of the church shall be kept as secret as possible. That no person under censure shall have a voice in the Church. That this covenant be READ at the admission of members, and that all things be done decently, and in order.

These things and whatsoever else we find contained in the Word of God, we (in a dependence on divine support) solemnly promise in the presence of almighty God to observe, and do, but knowing our insufficiency to do any things without divine help, we look up to the strong, for strength, and daily influence—Hold thou us up, O Lord, and we shall be safe, Amen.

THE SERAMPORE FORM
OF AGREEMENT (1805)[1]

Form of Agreement respecting the great principles upon which the Brethren of the Mission at Serampore think it their duty to act in the work of instructing the Heathen, agreed upon at a meeting of the Brethren at Serampore, on Monday, October 7, 1805.

The Redeemer, in planting us in this heathen nation, rather than in any other, has imposed upon us the cultivation of peculiar qualifications. We are firmly persuaded that Paul might plant and Apollos water, in vain, in any part of the world, did not God give the increase. We are sure that only those who are ordained to eternal life will believe, and that God alone can add to the Church such as shall be saved. Nevertheless we cannot but observe with admiration that Paul, the great champion for the glorious doctrines of free and sovereign grace, was the most conspicuous for his personal zeal in the work of persuading men to be reconciled to God. In

---

1   From "The Serampore Form of Agreement" as found in George Smith, *The Life of William Carey, D.D.: Shoemaker and Missionary* (London: John Murray, 1885), 441–50. The spelling and punctuation have been modernized.

this respect he is a noble example for our imitation. Our Lord intimated to those of his apostles who were fishermen, that he would make them fishers of men, intimating that in all weathers, and amidst every disappointment, they were to aim at drawing men to the shores of eternal life. Solomon says, "He that winneth souls is wise" [Proverbs 11:30], implying, no doubt, that the work of gaining over men to the side of God was to be done by winning methods, and that it required the greatest wisdom to do it with success. Upon these points, we think it right to fix our serious and abiding attention.

1. In order to be prepared for our great and solemn work, it is absolutely necessary that we set an infinite value upon immortal souls; that we often endeavor to affect our minds with the dreadful loss sustained by an unconverted soul launched into eternity. It becomes us to fix in our minds the awful doctrine of eternal punishment, and to realize frequently the inconceivably awful condition of this vast country, lying in the arms of the wicked one. If we have not this awful sense of the value of souls, it is impossible that we can feel aright in any other part of our work, and in this case it had been better for us to have been in any other situation rather than in that of a missionary. Oh! may our hearts bleed over these poor idolaters and may their case lie with continued weight on our minds, that we may resemble that eminent Missionary, who compared the travail of his soul, on account of the spiritual state of those committed to his charge, to the pains of childbirth. But while we thus mourn

over their miserable condition, we should not be discouraged, as though their recovery were impossible. He who raised the sottish and brutalized Britons to sit in heavenly places in Christ Jesus, can raise these slaves of superstition, purify their hearts by faith, and make them worshippers of the one God in spirit and in truth. The promises are fully sufficient to remove our doubts, and to make us anticipate that not very distant period when He will famish all the gods of India, and cause these very idolaters to cast their idols to the moles and to the bats, and renounce forever the work of their own hands.

2. It is very important that we should gain all the information we can of the snares and delusions in which these heathen are held. By this means we shall be able to converse with them in an intelligible manner. To know their modes of thinking, their habits, their propensities, their antipathies, the way in which they reason about God, sin, holiness, the way of salvation, and a future state, to be aware of the bewitching nature of their idolatrous worship, feasts, songs, etc., is of the highest consequence, if we would gain their attention to our discourse, and would avoid being barbarians to them. This knowledge may be easily obtained by conversing with sensible natives, by reading some parts of their works and by attentively observing their manners and customs.

3. It is necessary, in our intercourse with the Hindus, that, as far as we are able, we abstain from those things which would

increase their prejudices against the Gospel. Those parts of English manners which are most offensive to them should be kept out of sight as much as possible. We should also avoid every degree of cruelty to animals. Nor is it advisable at once to attack their prejudices by exhibiting with acrimony the sins of their gods; neither should we on any account do violence to their images, nor interrupt their worship. The real conquests of the Gospel are those of love: "And I, if I be lifted up, will draw all men unto me" [John 12:32]. In this respect, let us be continually fearful lest one unguarded word, or one unnecessary display of the difference betwixt us, in manners, etc., should set the natives at a greater distance from us. Paul's readiness to become all things to all men, that he might by any means save some and his disposition to abstain even from necessary comforts that he might not offend the weak, are circumstances worthy of our particular notice. This line of conduct we may be sure was founded on the wisest principles. Placed amidst a people very much like the hearers of the Apostle, in many respects, we may now perceive the solid wisdom which guided him as a missionary. The mild manners of the Moravians, and also of the Quakers, towards the North American Indians, have, in many instances, gained the affections and confidence of heathens in a wonderful manner. He who is too proud to stoop to others in order to draw them to him, though he may know that they are in many respects inferior to himself, is ill-qualified to become a missionary. The words of a most successful preacher of the Gospel still living, "that he would not care if the people trampled him under their feet, if he might become useful to their souls," are expressive of the very temper we should always cultivate.

4. It becomes us to watch all opportunities of doing good. A missionary would be highly culpable if he contented himself with preaching two or three times a week to those persons whom he might be able to get together into a place of worship. To carry on conversations with the natives almost every hour in the day, to go from village to village, from market to market, from one assembly to another, to talk to servants, laborers, etc., as often as opportunity offers, and to be instant in season and out of season, this is the life to which we are called in this country. We are apt to relax in these active exertions especially in a warm climate: but we shall do well always to fix in our minds that life is short, that all around us are perishing, and that we incur a dreadful woe if we proclaim not the glad tiding of salvation.

5. In preaching to the heathen, we must keep to the example of Paul, and make the great subject of our preaching, Christ the Crucified. It would be very easy for a missionary to preach nothing but truths, and that for many years together, without any well-grounded hope of becoming useful to one soul. The doctrine of Christ's expiatory death and all-sufficient merits has been, and must ever remain, the grand means of conversion. This doctrine, and others immediately connected with

it, have constantly nourished and sanctified the Church. Oh that these glorious truths may ever be the joy and strength of our own souls and then they will not fail to become the matter of our conversation to others. It was the proclaiming of these doctrines that made the Reformation from Popery in the time of Luther spread with such rapidity. It was these truths that filled the sermons of the modern apostles, Whitefield, Wesley, etc., when the light of the Gospel which had been held up with such glorious effects by the Puritans was almost extinguished in England. It is a well-known fact that the most successful missionaries in the world at the present day make the atonement of Christ their continued theme. We mean the Moravians. They attribute all their success to the preaching of the death of our Savior. So far as our experience goes in this work, we must freely acknowledge that every Hindu among us who has been gained to Christ, has been won by the astonishing and all-constraining love exhibited in our Redeemer's propitiatory death. O then may we resolve to know nothing among Hindus and Muslims but Christ and Him crucified.

6. It is absolutely necessary that the natives should have an entire confidence in us, and feel quite at home in our company. To gain this confidence we must on all occasions be willing to hear their complaints: we must give them the kindest advice: and we must decide upon everything brought before us in the most open, upright, and impartial manner.

We ought to be easy of access, to condescend to them as much as possible, and on all occasions to treat them as our equals. All passionate behavior will sink our characters exceedingly in their estimation. All force, and everything haughty, reserved and forbidding, it becomes us ever to shun with the greatest care. We can never make sacrifices too great, when the eternal salvation of souls is the object except, indeed, we sacrifice the commands of Christ.

7. Another important part of our work is to build up, and watch over, the souls that may be gathered. In this work we shall do well to simplify our first instructions as much as possible, and to press the great principles of the Gospel upon the minds of the converts till they be thoroughly settled and grounded in the foundation of their hope towards God. We must be willing to spend some time with them daily, if possible, in this work. We must have much patience with them, though they may grow very slowly in divine knowledge. We ought also to endeavor as much as possible to form them to habits of industry, and assist them in procuring such employments as may be pursued with the least danger of temptations to evil. Here too we shall have occasion to exercise much tenderness and forbearance, knowing that industrious habits are formed with difficulty by all heathen nations.

We ought also to remember that these persons have made no common sacrifices in renouncing their connections, their homes, their former situations and means of support, and that it will be very difficult for them to procure employment with heathen masters. In these circumstances, if we do not sympathize with them in their temporal losses for Christ, we shall be guilty of great cruelty.

As we consider it our duty to honor the civil magistrate, and in every state and country to render him the readiest obedience, whether we be persecuted or protected, it becomes us to instruct our native brethren in the same principles. A sense of gratitude too presses this obligation upon us in a peculiar manner in return for the liberal protection we have experienced. It is equally our wisdom and our duty also to show to the civil power, that it has nothing to fear from the progress of missions, since a real follower of Christ must resist the example of his great Master, and all the precepts the Bible contains on this subject, before he can become disloyal. Converted heathens, being brought over to the religion of their Christian Governors, if duly instructed, are much more likely to love them, and be united to them, than subjects of a different religion.

To bear the faults of our native brethren, so as to reprove them with tenderness, and set them right in the necessity of a holy conversation, is a very necessary duty. We should remember the gross darkness in which they were so lately involved, having never had any just and adequate ideas of the evil of sin or its consequences. We should also recollect how backward human nature is in forming spiritual ideas, and entering upon a holy self-denying conversation. We ought not, therefore, even after many falls, to give up and cast away a relapsed convert while he manifests the least inclination to be washed from his filthiness.

In walking before native converts, much care and circumspection are absolutely necessary. The falls of Christians in Europe have not such a fatal tendency as they must have in this country, because there the Word of God always commands more attention than the conduct of the most exalted Christian. But here those around us, in consequence of their little knowledge of the Scriptures, must necessarily take our conduct as a specimen of what Christ looks for in his disciples. They know only the Savior and his doctrine as they shine forth in us.

In conversing with the wives of native converts, and leading them on in the ways of Christ, so that they may be an ornament to the Christian cause, and make known the Gospel to the native women, we hope always to have the assistance of the females who have embarked with us in the mission. We see that in primitive times the Apostles were very much assisted in their great work by several pious females. The great value of female help may easily be appreciated if we consider how much the Asiatic women are shut up from the men, and especially from men of another caste. It behooves us therefore, to afford to our European sisters all possible assistance in acquiring the language, that they may, in every way which Providence may open to them, become instrumental in promoting the salvation of the millions of native women who are in a great measure excluded from all opportunities of hearing the Word from the mouths of European missionaries. A European sister may do much for the cause in this respect, by promoting the holiness, and stirring up the zeal, of the female native converts. A real missionary becomes in a sense a father to his people. If he feel all the anxiety and tender solicitude of a father, all that delight in their welfare and company that a father does in the midst of his children, they will feel all that freedom with, and confidence in him which he can desire. He will be wholly unable to lead them on in a regular and happy manner, unless they can be induced to open their minds to him, and unless a sincere and mutual esteem subsist on both sides.

8. Another part of our work is the forming of our native brethren to usefulness, fostering every kind of genius, and cherishing every gift and grace in them. In this respect we can scarcely be too lavish of our attention to their improvement. It is only by means of native preachers that we can hope for the universal spread of the Gospel throughout this immense continent. Europeans are too few, and their subsistence costs too much for us ever to hope that they can possibly be the instruments of the universal diffusion of the Word amongst so many millions of souls spread over such a large portion of the habitable globe. Their incapability of bearing the intense heat of the climate in perpetual itineracies, and the heavy expenses of their journeys, not to say anything of the prejudices of the

natives against the very presence of Europeans, and the great difficulty of becoming fluent in their languages, render it an absolute duty to cherish native gifts, and to send forth as many native preachers as possible. If the practice of confining the ministry of the Word to a single individual in a Church be once established amongst us, we despair of the Gospel's ever making much progress in India by our means. Let us therefore use every gift, and continually urge on our native brethren to press upon their countrymen the glorious Gospel of the blessed God.

Still further to strengthen the cause of Christ in this country, and as far as in our power, to give it a permanent establishment, even when the efforts of Europeans may fail, we think it our duty, as soon as possible, to advise the native brethren who may be formed into separate Churches to choose their pastors and deacons from amongst their own countrymen, that the Word may be statedly preached, and the ordinances of Christ administered, in each Church by the native minister, as much as possible without the interference of the missionary of the district who will constantly super-intend their affairs, give them advice in cases of order and discipline, and correct any errors into which they may fall, and who joying and beholding their order, and the steadfast-ness of their faith in Christ, may direct his efforts continually to the planting of new Churches in other places, and to the spread of the Gospel throughout his district as much as in his power. By this means the unity of the missionary character will be preserved, all the missionaries will still form one body, each one moveable as the good of the cause may require; the different native Churches will also naturally learn to care and provide for their ministers, for their Church expenses, the raising of places of worship, etc., and the whole administration will assume a native aspect; by which means the inhabitants will more readily identify the cause as belonging to their own nation, and their prejudices at falling into the hands of Europeans will entirely vanish. It may be hoped too that the pastors of these Churches, and the members in general, will feel a new energy in attempting to spread the Gospel, when they shall thus freely enjoy the privileges of the Gospel amongst themselves. Under the divine blessing, if in the course of a few years a number of native Churches be thus established, from them the Word of God may sound out even to the extremities of India; and numbers of preachers being raised up and sent forth, may form a body of native missionaries, inured to the climate, acquainted with the customs, language, modes of speech, and reasoning of the inhabitants; able to become perfectly familiar with them, to enter their houses, to live upon their food, to sleep with them, or under a tree; and who may travel from one end of the country to the other almost without any expense. These Churches will be in no immediate danger of falling into errors or disorders, because the whole of their affairs will be constantly superintended by a European missionary. The advantages of this plan are so evident, that to carry it into complete effect ought to be our continued concern. That we may discharge the important obligations of watching over these infant churches when formed, and of urging them to maintain a steady discipline, to hold forth the clear and cheering light of evangelical truth in this region and shadow of death, and to walk in all respects as those who have been called out of darkness into marvelous light, we should go continually to the Source of all grace and strength; for if, to become the shepherd of one Church be a most solemn and weighty charge, what must it be to watch over a number of Churches just raised from a state of heathenism, and placed at a distance from each other.

We have thought it our duty not to change the names of native converts, observing from Scripture that the Apostles did not change those of the first Christians turned from heathenism, as the names Epaphroditus, Phoebe, Fortunatus, Sylvanus, Apollos, Hermes, Junia, Narcissus, etc., prove. Almost all these names are derived from those of heathen gods. We think the great object which divine Providence has in view in causing the Gospel to be promulgated in the world, is not the changing of the names, the dress, the food, and the innocent usages of mankind, but to produce a moral and divine change in the hearts and conduct of men. It would not be right to perpetuate the names of heathen gods amongst Christians; neither is it necessary or prudent to give a new name to every man after his conversion, as hereby the economy of families, neighborhoods, etc., would be needlessly disturbed.

In other respects we think it our duty to lead our brethren by example, by mild persuasion, and by opening and illuminating their minds in a gradual way, rather than use authoritative means. By this they learn to see the evil of a custom, and then to despise and forsake it; whereas in cases where force is used, though they may leave off that which is wrong while in our presence, yet not having seen the evil of it, they are in danger of using hypocrisy, and of doing that out of our presence which they dare not do in it.

9. It becomes us also to labor with all our might in forwarding translations of the sacred Scriptures in the languages of Hindustan. The help which God has already afforded us in this work is a loud call to us to "go forward." So far, therefore, as God has qualified us to learn those languages which are necessary, we consider it our bounden duty to apply with unwearied assiduity in acquiring them. We consider the publication of the divine Word throughout India as an object which we ought never to give up till accomplished, looking to the Fountain of all knowledge and strength, to qualify us for this great work, and to carry us through it to the praise of his holy name.

It becomes us to use all assiduity in explaining and distributing the divine Word on all occasions, and by every means in our power to excite the attention and reverence of the natives towards it, as the fountain of eternal truth, and the message of salvation to men. It is our duty also to distribute, as extensively as possible, the different religious tracts which are published. Considering how much the general diffusion of the knowledge of Christ depends upon a constant and liberal distribution of the Word, and of these tracts all over the country, we should keep this continually in mind, and watch all opportunities of putting even single tracts into the hands of those persons with whom we occasionally meet. We should endeavor to ascertain where large assemblies of natives are to be found, that we may attend upon them, and gladden whole villages at once with the tidings of salvation.

The establishment of native free schools is also an object highly important to the future conquests of the Gospel. Of this very pleasing and interesting part of our missionary labors we should endeavor not to be unmindful. As opportunities are afforded, it becomes us to establish, visit, and encourage these institutions, and to recommend the establishment of them to other Europeans. The progress of divine light is gradual, both as it respects individuals and nations. Whatever therefore tends to increase the body of holy light in these dark regions, is as bread cast upon the waters, to be seen after many days. In many ways the progress of providential events is preparing the Hindus for casting their idols to the moles and the bats, and for becoming a part of the chosen generation, the royal priesthood, the holy nation. Some parts of missionary labors very properly tend to the present conversion of the heathen, and others to the ushering in of the glorious period when a nation shall be born in a day. Of the latter are native free schools.

10. That which, as a means, is to fit us for the discharge of these laborious and unutterably important labors, is the being instant in prayer, and the cultivation of personal religion. Let us ever have in remembrance the examples of those who have been most eminent in the work of God. Let us often look at Brainerd in the woods of America, pouring out his very soul before God for the perishing heathen, without whose salvation nothing could make him happy. Prayer—secret, fervent, believing prayer—lies at the root of all personal godliness. A competent knowledge of the languages where a missionary lives, a mild and winning temper, and a heart given up to God in closest religion, these, these are the attainments which, more than all knowledge or all other gifts, will fit us to become the instruments of God in the great work of human redemption. Let us then ever be united in prayer at stated seasons, whatever distance may separate us, and let each one of us lay it upon his heart that we will seek to be fervent in spirit, wrestling with God, till He famish these idols, and cause the heathen to experience the blessedness that is in Christ. Finally, let us give ourselves unreservedly to this glorious cause. Let us never think that our time, our gifts, our strength, our families, or even the clothes we wear, are our own. Let us sanctify them all to God and His cause. Oh that he may sanctify us for his work. Let us forever shut out the idea of laying up a cowrie for ourselves or our children. If we give up the resolution which was formed on the subject of private trade when we first united at Serampore, the mission is from that hour a

lost cause. A worldly spirit, quarrels, and every evil work will succeed the moment it is admitted that each brother may do something on his own account. Woe to that man who shall ever make the smallest movement toward such a measure! Let us continually watch against a worldly spirit, and cultivate a Christian indifference towards every indulgence. Rather let us bear hardness as good soldiers of Jesus Christ and endeavor to learn in every state to be content.

If in this way we are enabled to glorify God with our bodies and spirits which are his, our wants will be his care. No private family ever enjoyed a greater portion of happiness, even in the most prosperous gale of worldly prosperity, than we have done since we resolved to have all things in common and that no one should pursue business for his own exclusive advantage. If we are enabled to persevere in the same principles, we may hope that multitudes of converted souls will have reason to bless God to all eternity for sending his Gospel into this country.

To keep these ideas alive in our minds, we resolve that this agreement shall be read publicly, at every station, at our three annual meetings, viz. on the first Lord's day in January, in May and October.

William Carey
Joshua Marshman
William Ward
John Chamberlain

John Bliss
William Moore
Joshua Rowe
Felix Carey
Richard Mardon
Mission House, Serampore

INDEX

ABOUT THE AUTHOR

Dr. Michael A.G. Haykin is chair and professor of church history and biblical spirituality at The Southern Baptist Theological Seminary in Louisville, Ky., where he serves as director of the Andrew Fuller Center for Baptist Studies. He is also a fellow of the Royal Historical Society in the United Kingdom.

Born in England of Irish and Kurdish parents, Dr. Haykin earned a B.A. in philosophy from the University of Toronto and an M.Rel. and a Th.D. from Wycliffe College and the University of Toronto. He is author of numerous books, including *Rediscovering the Church Fathers: Who They Were and How They Shaped the Church*, *The Christian Lover: The Sweetness of Love and Marriage in the Letters of Believers*, and *Jonathan Edwards: The Holy Spirit in Revival*. He is currently involved as the general editor of a seventeen-volume critical edition of the works of Andrew Fuller.